Vegan Diet for Athletes

The Complete Vegan Solution for Athletes and fitness Enthusiasts with 150 Easy High-Protein Recipes to Strengthen Your Body

Jesica Haren

© **Copyright 2020 – By Jesica Haren All Rights Reserved.**

This book is copyright protected. It is only for personal use. You cannot amend, distribute, sell, use, quote or paraphrase any part of the content within this book, without the consent of the author or publisher.

Under no circumstances will any blame or legal responsibility be held against the publisher, or author, for any damages, reparation, or monetary loss due to the information contained within this book, either directly or indirectly.

Disclaimer Notice:

Please note the information contained within this document is for educational and entertainment purposes only. All effort has been executed to present accurate, up to date, reliable, complete information. No warranties of any kind are declared or implied. Readers acknowledge that the author is not engaged in the rendering of legal, financial, medical or professional advice. The content within this book has been derived from various sources. Please consult a licensed professional before attempting any techniques outlined in this book.

By reading this document, the reader agrees that under no circumstances is the author responsible for any losses, direct or indirect, that are incurred as a result of the use of the information contained within this document, including, but not limited to, errors, omissions, or inaccuracies.

Content

1   Introduction

Part I

3   **Chapter 1:** The Plant-Based Diet for Athletes

Part II The Recipe

32   **Chapter 2:** Breakfast and Smoothies
42   **Chapter 3:** Pre-Training Meals
47   **Chapter 4:** Midday Meals
61   **Chapter 5:** Post-Training Meals
74   **Chapter 6:** Snacks and Sides
87   **Chapter 7:** Dinner
100   **Chapter 8:** Desserts
108   **Chapter 9:** Staples, Sauces and Dressings

118   *Appendix 1:* ***Measurement Conversion Chart***
119   *Appendix 2:* ***Recipe Index***
121   ***References***

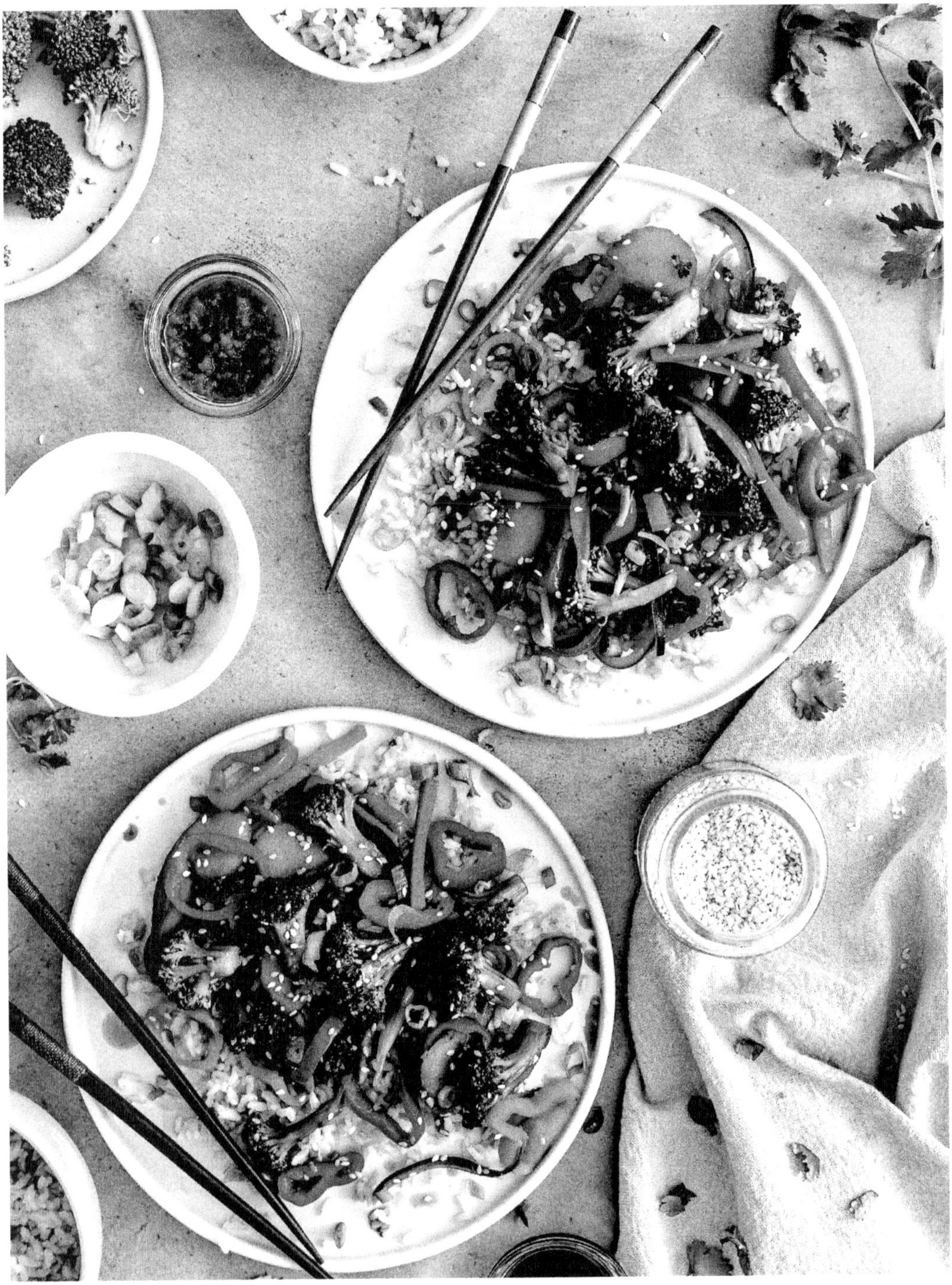

Introduction

Sports have been a significant part of my life since I was a child. My time as an athlete has helped me to grow to be a better person and feel more comfortable in my skin, at least that's what I like to believe. It's taught me discipline, the value of hard work, and how great it feels to be part of a team.

As an adult, I had to limit the number of sports I was involved in, mainly due to time constraints, but cycling, swimming, and running remained firm favorites. Triathlons soon became a natural progression, and I have competed at a semi-professional level for several years now.

As a developing athlete, I was always told along with most athletes, that protein is the most vital part of our diet, and as such, I made sure to include some form of meat in almost all my meals. Around my mid-20s, I felt myself start to lag in performance. It didn't make sense to me because I was competing with athletes who were far older than I was, and they were still breaking records and making podium finishes. One day after a particularly grueling triathlon event, I was close to giving up. Although I felt like going home and throwing in the towel for good, I decided to stay for the medal ceremony, and I am so glad I did!

The gold medalist was a female athlete, probably around 35 years old. I approached her to congratulate her, and, on a whim, explained how I felt like I was going backward in my performance. I asked her what her secret was, and although I had heard the word 'vegan' before, I was pretty sure that athletes could not be vegan. I mean, where would you get enough protein? That conversation changed my life and my performance, and to this day, I advocate a vegan or whole-food plant-based diet to any athlete I know.

Although it took some time for me to settle into a good rhythm and understand the concept of moderation and balance, within weeks of starting on a vegan or whole-food plant-based (WFPB) diet, I saw a huge difference in my performance.

I had more energy overall, I recovered quicker after particularly arduous events, I was sleeping better, and my mental focus was hugely improved. Through my research, I began to understand that by including so much meat and other animal products in my diet, I was essentially slowing down my digestive system. As a result, despite thinking I was eating a pretty healthy diet, I could not get the nutrition my body needed. On a WFPB diet, I was able to train for longer, I generally felt strong, and my muscle mass was maintained even when I took breaks. This enormous improvement in my athletic performance and overall health was such a revelation that I had to share it.

Chapter 1

The Plant-Based Diet for Athletes

I guess one of the reasons that I initially struggled to equate a vegan or WFPB diet with the life of an athlete was because the whole idea of plant-based nutrition summoned images of plates of lettuce or bags of carrot sticks in my mind. Of course, that is societal conditioning, just like the idea that we need animal products to meet our protein needs. Once I managed to get past that skewed thinking, the reality made so much sense.

Plant-based nutrition is based on the principles that the most nutritionally valuable foods are not heavily processed. They are whole or minimally refined. In addition to this, plant-based sources are, of course, foods that do not contain any form of animal products, including meat, eggs, milk, or honey. One of the things that put people off this diet is that it seems restrictive, but the truth is that it is only your perception of the range of limited plant-based foods. The range of foods included in a plant-based diet include:

- Vegetables and fruit
- Tubers (roots like potatoes and beets)
- Legumes (beans, pulses, and lentils)
- Whole Grains (cereals, grains, and starches like brown rice, whole wheat, oats, barley, quinoa, and even popcorn)
- Other plant-based sources (seeds, nuts, and plant milk)

As the vegan or plant-based community has grown, the range of products that cater to this diet has expanded exponentially, and today, there is almost no limitation to what you can eat that is of plant-based origin. It is important to be careful when buying meat-imitation products, though, like vegan sausages or vegan burger patties, as often these contain high levels of flavorings and other chemicals, and, as a result, they are almost as unhealthy as any other processed food.

Switching over to plant-based nutrition doesn't need to be an overnight thing. In fact, I recommend that you make small incremental changes as you work toward your goal. This will help you stay on track and not feel like you are "missing out" on anything. Even when you are predominantly switched over, if you feel like having a slice of cheese or an egg, do it. The idea is not to restrict or punish yourself. You are benefiting from the decision to switch over to a plant-based diet, so it should never feel like a chore. The great thing is that the more you can include plant-based foods in your diet, the less you will feel like eating animal products.

Much of what we eat is not about taste or preference but actually about habit, and all you need to do is change the habit.

Catering to Athletic Needs With Plant-Based Nutrition

In figuring out exactly how to cater to your athletic needs through plant-based nutrition, the first thing to consider is the type of athlete you are? Different athletic disciplines require different types of nutritional intakes, so this is where we start:

- Short Duration Event Athletes: 60% carbohydrates, 15-25% fat, and 15-25% protein
- Intermediate Duration Event Athletes: 55-60% carbohydrates, 15-20% fat, and 15-25%
- Long Duration Event Athletes: 60-70% carbohydrates, 20-30% fat, and 10-15% protein (Weatherwax-Fall, n.d.)

One thing should stand out for you here, and that is how, regardless of your event duration, protein requirements are a lot less important than we've been made to believe. In almost all athletic disciplines, protein is either the least important macronutrient or equally as vital as fat.

Once you have determined how you should be structuring your diet for your particular discipline, the next step is to figure out the best plant-based sources of these macronutrients.

Carbohydrate Sources

When you think about carbohydrates in plants, you probably only think about potatoes, or maybe corn. You will be surprised to discover that almost all plant-based foods contain some carbohydrates. Your best plant-based carbohydrate sources are:

- Fruits
- Vegetables with starch like potatoes and squash
- Whole Grains

Protein Sources

Your best plant-based protein sources are:

- Lentils
- Beans
- Seeds
- Quinoa
- Nuts
- Tofu
- Spirulina

Fat Sources

Your best plant-based fat sources are:

- Oils
- Avocado
- Seeds
- Nuts
- Nut Butters

The whole-foods component of this diet means that you want to avoid any heavily processed food. Depending on what your diet looks like now, switching over to plant-based nutrition may seem challenging in the beginning. The key here is to make a gradual and determined switch, and give yourself space for treats and cheats now and then. If you attempt to rigorously and strictly switch yourself over to a plant-based diet overnight without any leeway or allowances, you will very likely fail. You know yourself better than anyone, and you know what animal products or processed foods will be difficult to give up, so focus on those first. If you have a sweet tooth, and you can't imagine your life without a daily chocolate bar, start working on that challenge first.

Find as many plant-based whole-food sources of sugar to replace your chocolate and stock up on those. Then allow yourself one small chocolate bar per week. You will be amazed at how quickly you struggle to finish a sweet that you once devoured with no problem.

Every positive change you make is a healthy one, so keep that in mind throughout your journey. Other problem areas that are similar to sugar addictions are alcohol and caffeine. If you are used to a mixed drink every night, try to swap that out for a glass of red wine instead. Red wine contains antioxidants and has been linked to easier weight maintenance. If caffeine is your Achilles Heel, don't worry. Although consuming huge amounts of coffee or caffeine in other sources is not healthy, coffee in moderation is very good for you. It works toward helping to maintain your weight in the same way red wine does, and it also helps your liver heal itself.

The Paradox of Meat Eating and Performance

As we notice more competitive and professional athletes switching over to a plant-based diet and seeing improved performance, we have to question the old assumption that athletes need animal protein and dairy to build muscle.

If you still aren't convinced that you can be vegan and be a successful athlete, the following is a list of 14 athletes who have switched to a vegan lifestyle and maintained or improved their performance:

1. **Venus Williams** - Winner of seven grand slams singles titles and 14 doubles titles, Venus has also won Wimbledon five times and has four Olympic gold medals. She has been vegan since 2011.

2. **Lewis Hamilton** - Hamilton has been crowned the world champion in Formula 1 four times and is the 10th highest-paid athlete in the world. He has been vegan since 2017.

3. **Scott Jurek -** Jurek is a long-distance marathon runner and has won 16 ultramarathon titles. His vegan journey started when he was in college.

4. **Jermain Defoe -** English professional footballer, Defoe has scored over 150 goals in the Premier League, making him the seventh-best all-time goalscorer in the League's history.

5. **David Haye -** British boxer, Haye, has won two world titles in two different weight categories. He has been vegan for four years after researching the faster healing times experienced on a plant-based diet.

6. **Barny du Plessis -** This bodybuilder won the Mr. Universe title in 2014, and he is the world's first vegan professional bodybuilder. He had to retire in 2013 due to a wide range of health issues, but after switching over to a vegan diet, he could return to his sport and be even more successful than before.

7. **Hannah Teter -** Teter is a snowboarder and has won three Olympic medals. She has lived a vegetarian lifestyle for most of her life but switched over to veganism in 2010.

8. **Kendrick Farris -** Weightlifter, Farris, is an Olympian and has been a vegan since the birth of his second son.

9. **Tia Blanco -** This professional surfer has won the Women's Open twice, and although she grew up as a vegetarian, she switched over to veganism entirely in 2013.

10. **Nate Diaz -** Diaz is a mixed martial artist and competes professionally in the UFC. He has been a vegan since the age of 18 and feels that it improves his mental focus during fights.

11. **Meagan Duhamel -** This four-time world pairs ice skating champion is also an Olympic medalist. She has won two Four Continents Championships and six Canadian National Championships. She has been a vegan since 2008.

12. **Timothy Shieff** - Shieff is a free runner and switched over to veganism after suffering from mild tendonitis. With the promise of faster healing times, he tried the diet and was so impressed with his improved performance; he stuck with it.

13. **Jack Lindquist** - This track cyclist adopted a vegan diet in 2005 for personal reasons, and saw a dramatic improvement in his performance. Lindquist now blogs about his sport as well as the benefits of veganism for athletes.

14. **Abel Trujillo** - This mixed martial arts fighter is 'affectionately' nicknamed 'Killa,' and he credits every fighting title he has won to his vegan lifestyle.

The World Health Organization has classified processed meat as a carcinogen, meaning it is likely to cause cancer. The truth is that there is significant evidence to indicate that all meat has this effect. Large studies conducted in the UK have shown that people on a plant-based diet are 40% less likely to develop cancer (Krantz, 2016). Meat consumption also significantly increases the risk of other chronic illnesses like cardiovascular disease and diabetes. Most chronic diseases result from chronic inflammation in the cells of the affected area. When we digest meat, our body produces a compound called trimethylamine oxide (TMAO), which has been linked by several studies to chronic inflammation. Some proponents of meat-containing diets will claim that grass-fed meat does not have this effect. This has been scientifically disproven, and we now know that regardless of what an animal eats throughout its life, its meat has the same impact on the human body when consumed.

The link between obesity and meat consumption is also well-established by meat-eaters being three times more likely to be obese than vegetarians. High levels of hormones and antibiotics in meat are also hazardous. Interestingly the fish and shellfish we eat today often have the same effect on us as meat does. Farming of fish and shellfish to retain sustainable numbers has resulted in an aquaculture industry that treats the fish they are farming the same way that livestock is treated in the animal agriculture industry. Fish are fed antibiotics, hormones, and growth-promoting foods to increase their size and speed up growth.

With all of these negative side effects from meat-eating, and the knowledge that it is entirely possible to get the same amount of protein from plant-based sources, is there really any question about whether going plant-based is a good idea?

The myth that athletes require animal protein and dairy to perform well continues to persist even within groups of athletes. Many professional athletes that have moved over to a plant-based diet have reported teasing and ridicule from their fellow athletes in the early stages of their journey. Derek Tresize is a bodybuilder and the owner of Root Force Personal Training in Virginia. He reports that when first switching to a vegan diet, he was heavily ridiculed by his peers, but that soon faded when his performance improved, and he began to gain more muscle than his carnivorous peers (Gerard, n.d.).

The Benefits of a WFPB Diet

A whole-food plant-based diet is not just beneficial from an athletic perspective. This diet provides significant health benefits over and above performance levels. These benefits include:

- The prevention and reversal of chronic diseases
- Improved metabolic health and constitution
- Weight loss and management becomes far easier
- Indulging in larger portions is no longer a major issue
- The guilt-free enjoyment of food that has not harmed any other living creature
- Improved complexion, natural body scent, and sexual health
- Increased energy levels
- Improved mental health and overall mood
- Better sleep
- Greater longevity

Overall a WFPB diet better serves our nutritional needs for:

- Energy requirements
- Endurance levels
- Strength building and maintenance
- Faster recovery from injuries and rigorous workouts
- Improved rest and sleep quality
- Sharper mental focus

Macro Nutritional Needs for Athletes

Protein

Although not the holy grail that it is made out to be, athletes require higher protein levels than non-athletes. This is mostly to help repair and build muscle after training. Most athletes should be eating about 20 to 40 grams of protein every four hours. The following salad contains about 24 grams of protein:

- ¼ cup of nuts
- ½ cup of chickpeas
- 6 ounces of tofu
- Some vegetables

The following are some other high-quality protein sources that should be included throughout the day and their protein content per ½ cup serving (unless otherwise stated).

- Lentils (9 grams)
- Tempeh (15 grams)
- Chickpeas (7 grams)
- Mycoprotein (13 grams)
- Quinoa (8 grams)
- Chia seeds (2 grams per tablespoon)
- Hemp seeds (5 grams per tablespoon)
- Peanuts (20.5 grams)
- Almonds (16.5 grams)
- Spirulina (8 grams)
- Beans and rice (3.5 grams)
- Buckwheat (3 grams)
- Potato (one large baked potato contains 8 grams of protein)
- Amaranth (5 grams)
- Broccoli (one single stalk contains 4 grams of protein)
- Kale (1 gram)
- Mushrooms (5 mushrooms contain 3 grams of protein)
- Seitan (31.5 grams)
- Ezekiel bread (4 grams per slice)
- Edamame (8.5 grams)
- Soy yogurt (10 grams)
- Soy Milk (4 grams)
- Tofu (10 grams)

Most whole-foods, including broccoli, kale, beans, and spinach, have 15% or higher protein content. Vegetables are a higher source of protein than fruit. The key to maintaining a healthy protein intake as a vegan is to ensure that you are not merely replacing animal sources with plant sources, but still eating processed foods. If you eat a vegan diet and still include high levels of sugar and oil, for instance, you will likely struggle to consume sufficient levels of protein. Essentially, you do not want to just replace non-vegan products with vegan products; your diet needs to shift to include more whole-foods to be nutritious.

Animal Protein Versus Plant Protein

The human body requires nine different amino acids to function correctly. Amino acids are formed when protein is broken down in the body. When a protein source contains all nine amino acids, it is considered 'complete.' Many animal protein sources are complete, as well as several plant-based protein sources. A few plant-based protein sources are incomplete, though, so it is important to know which ones.

The following plant proteins are considered complete:

- Quinoa
- Buckwheat
- Soy
- Mycoprotein
- Rice and beans
- Ezekiel bread
- Seitan
- Hummus
- Spirulina with grains and nuts
- Peanut butter on whole-wheat bread

Incomplete plant proteins include hemp seeds and chia. With the wide range of complete plant-based protein sources available, you should have no problem getting in the amount of protein you need. Amino acids are just one part of a wide network of nutritional requirements that our bodies have, and the negative aspects of eating animal protein far outweigh any considerations regarding amino acids. The best way to avoid any deficiencies in amino acids when you are on a plant-based diet is to eat a wide range of protein sources. If you are going to try and use lentils as your only protein source on a plant-based diet, you will make yourself ill. In the same way, it stands to reason that if you only ate steak, you would also not be healthy.

Carbohydrates

Carbohydrates are another macronutrient given a bad name seemingly for no reason, specifically by the weight loss industry. The truth, though, is that not all carbohydrates are created equal. While you definitely want to avoid refined carbohydrates like cakes and cookies, complex carbohydrates are different. As athletes, about 60% of our total calories should be made up of carbohydrates.

The following are some sources of healthy plant-based complex carbohydrates and their carbohydrate content per ½ cup serving:

- Oats (23 grams)
- Sweet potatoes (14 grams)
- Quinoa (20 grams)
- Prunes (56 grams)
- Pulses (11 grams)
- Pumpkin (4 grams)
- Buckwheat (50 grams)
- Cherries (11 grams)
- Taro (14 grams)
- Beets (8 grams)
- Soy yogurt (21 grams)
- Cassava (39 grams)
- Bananas (26 grams)
- Carrots (7 grams)

Fats

Like carbohydrates, fats have been given a bad reputation by the weight loss community, and the claims of low-fat products being healthier are based in no science at all. Again like carbohydrates, it is the type of fat you consume that makes all the difference.

As an athlete, you will need about 22 to 35% of your daily caloric intake to be made up of fat, depending on your discipline.

In general, there are two types of fat—saturated and unsaturated. While these can be split up into various types and aren't too bad in small quantities, generally saturated fats are to be avoided in large amounts, and unsaturated fats are the ones we want to predominantly include.

The following are some sources of plant-based unsaturated fats and how many grams of fat they deliver per ½ cup:

- Walnuts (52 grams)
- Avocados (20 grams)
- Nut butter (48 grams)
- Cacao nibs (32 grams)
- Flaxseeds (120 grams)
- Olives (26 grams)
- Seed butter (40 grams)
- Tofu (10 grams)
- Edamame (3 grams)

Cut Out the Oil

In reading the above list, you may get the idea that you could use the oil of a good source of unsaturated fat instead of the source itself. While that is not entirely incorrect, using avocado oil instead of eating avocado or using olive oil instead of eating olives, you are losing out on all the micronutrients in the food source itself.

Oils are often heavily processed and high in calories, whereas the food source is high nutrients and lower in empty calories. In weight loss or weight maintenance routines, you really want to try and cut out as many empty calories as possible. For every calorie you take in, you want to account for a good intake of macro and micronutrients as well.

The following list is a rough guide of the number of calories per pound of a specific food source. This list is vital in terms of ensuring that you are taking in enough nutritious calories. When trying to lose weight, it is best to focus on foods at the top of the list, and simultaneously reduce your oil intake.

- Vegetables (100 calories)
- Fruits (300 calories)
- Unrefined complex carbohydrates such as legumes, potatoes, and whole grains (400 to 600 calories)
- Avocados (750 calories)
- Refined complex carbohydrates (1,200 calories)
- Sugar (1,800 calories)
- Chocolate (2,500 calories)
- Nuts and seeds (2,800 calories)
- Oil (4,000 calories)

How to Reduce Oil Consumption

The thought of reducing your oil intake might automatically take your mind to all the foods you think you can no longer prepare. Rest assured, though, that there are many ways to continue cooking your favorite fried foods without using oil:

- Gradually switch over to a cooking spray to replace oil.
- Use nonstick cookware to negate the need for oil.
- Use water, vegetable puree, or broth as a substitute for oil.
- Put your oil into a spray bottle so that instead of pouring large glugs of oil, you are using only a fine mist.
- Consider purchasing an air fryer, which will fry your food with superheated air and only a slight misting of oil.

The Importance of Micronutrients

The name of this group of vitamins and minerals belies their importance in our overall health. A deficiency in any micronutrient can cause major health problems, and as athletes, it can seriously affect performance.

Some of the processes that micronutrients support include:

- Oxygen transport across red blood cell
- The conversion of food into energy
- Building strong bones and teeth

The ease with which our body can take in specific vitamins and minerals from different sources is bioavailability. Bioavailability is a major factor in the source we use for our micronutrients. For instance, calcium is more bioavailable in milk than it is in spinach, so as plant-based athletes, we need to slightly adjust the amount of plant-based sources we take in to make up for this. More importantly, we should ensure that we have a very diverse plant-based diet to increase our chances of taking up the micronutrients we need.

Vitamins

Vitamins are divided into two types:

- **Water-soluble:** these vitamins, including B and C, are soluble in the blood without any fat present.

- **Fat-soluble:** these vitamins, A, D, K, and E, are soluble only with fat (lipids), so if you have an extremely low-fat diet, you may experience difficulty in absorbing these vitamins.

Understanding how the body absorbs the different vitamins highlights the importance of eating a balanced diet. If you are cutting down too much on fat, you risk not properly absorbing fat-soluble vitamins from your food and developing a deficiency.

Vitamins serve different functions in our bodies, and can be taken up from various plant sources:

- **Vitamin A** is needed to maintain eyesight and be found in orange and yellow vegetables and fruits and leafy green vegetables.

- **Vitamin B** consists of a family of vitamins including B1, 2, 3, 5, 6, 7, 9, and 12. They have various functions in the body like managing stress, nervousness, anxiety, and insomnia, so we need to ensure a constant supply. The best plant-based sources for B-vitamins include the germ of a whole grain and the bran of rice husks and wheat. Vitamin B12 is possibly the most important of these vitamins and aids the nervous system in supporting energy requirements and longevity. This is one of the few vitamins that are not sufficiently bioavailable in a plant-based diet, and in a later section, we will discuss how this can easily be corrected with supplements. Fermented foods are a great source of vitamin B12.

- **Folic acid,** also known as vitamin B9, is essential for certain body functions and the formation of red blood cells. It is also used in brain functioning and development. Good plant-based sources of folic acid include green, leafy vegetables like beet greens, spinach, and kale.

- **Vitamin C** is an immune system booster that helps to build connective tissue and support the adrenal system. Plant-based vitamin C sources include cantaloupe, strawberries, peppers, cabbage, tomatoes, citrus fruits, and green, leafy vegetables.

- **Vitamin D** is essential for the immune system and bone health, and although, in food sources, it is predominantly found in animal-based foods, it is entirely possible to get on a plant-based diet. This is one of the few vitamins that can be absorbed through the skin, and 15 to 30 minutes of exposure to sunlight per day is sufficient for our needs. This doesn't mean you have to bask in the sun as activities like gardening, sitting outside reading a book, or taking a walk are good ways to reach your vitamin D quota. In winter, you may want to consider taking a supplement.

- **Vitamin E** is also an antioxidant and helps prevent damage to cells and slow down the aging process. Its best plant-based sources are nuts, grains, and seeds.

Minerals

Minerals are naturally-occurring compounds that can be found in a wide range of sources. They play a vital role in the function and health of various areas of the body. The following are some of the most important minerals, their functions, and the plant-based sources they can be acquired from.

- **Calcium:** This mineral is vital for bone health, muscle suppleness, as well as the transporting of messages through nerve endings to the brain. The best plant-based sources for calcium are green, leafy vegetables, broccoli, tofu, sunflower seeds, chickpeas, beans, dried fruit, dried figs, sesame seeds, and blackstrap molasses.

- **Chromium:** This trace mineral helps to improve insulin sensitivity and enhances the metabolism of macronutrients. Its best plant-based sources are whole grains, peanuts, nuts, cooked spinach, broccoli, apples, and mushrooms.
- **Copper:** This essential mineral helps to maintain a healthy metabolism, improves bone health, and ensures that the nervous system is working correctly. The best plant-based sources for copper include seeds, whole grains, nuts, mushrooms, and dried beans.
- **Fluoride:** This element is required in very small amounts in the body and is predominantly important in bones and teeth strength, which is why it is often added to toothpaste. Plant-based sources of fluoride include apples, brewed tea, cooked spinach, and kale.
- **Iodine:** This mineral is important in thyroid hormone functioning, which helps to maintain the metabolism. It is predominantly found in plant-based sources like sea salt, iodine-rich sea vegetables, iodized salt, and kelp.
- **Iron:** This is probably one of the most important minerals, and it serves to ensure that red blood cells can carry oxygen throughout our bodies. Plant-based iron sources include sea vegetables, legumes, seeds, green leafy vegetables, watermelon, bran flakes, prune juice, and dried fruit.
- **Magnesium:** This mineral helps to regulate muscle and nerve function, making it very important for athletes. It is most commonly found in plant-based sources like brown rice, cooked spinach, almonds, beans, wheat bran, dried figs, bananas, and peanuts.
- **Manganese:** This helps to activate enzymes in metabolic processes and to breakdown proteins and amino acids. The best plant-based sources of manganese include cooked oatmeal, black beans, cooked kale, avocados, strawberries, and pineapple.
- **Phosphorus:** As well as being involved in the formation of strong bones and teeth, it is also vital in how the body uses fats and carbohydrates. The best plant-based phosphorus sources include bread and baked goods, cereal grains, nuts, lentils, pinto beans, brown rice, spinach, avocados, yeast, and vegetables.

- **Potassium:** This mineral helps regulate fluid balance in the body, and controls muscle contractions vital for athletes. It can be found in bananas, normal and sweet potatoes, raisins, winter squash, spinach, kiwi, dried fruit, dried apricots, melons, grapefruit, and strawberries.
- **Zinc:** This mineral is vital for the proper functioning of the immune system and the manufacturer of proteins and DNA in the body. The best plant-based sources for zinc include pumpkin seeds, whole grains, cereals, legumes, lentils, garbanzo beans, sunflower seeds, yeast, maple syrup, raw collard greens, and corn.

Foods That Are Good to Eat Every Day

As you have gathered by now, the key to getting in all of the macro and micronutrients you need as an athlete is to eat a varied diet and include as many different foods as possible. Some foods are important to include in your daily diet.

Fruits

I have found that the absolute easiest way to increase my fruit intake is at breakfast. Smoothies are great to include both fruits and vegetables, as well as a nice addition to breakfast cereal or yogurt.

Berries are the superfood of the fruit family containing huge amounts of antioxidants. Strawberries also contain sirtuin-activating components. Sirtuin genes improve our metabolism and make weight maintenance easier. If you only think of strawberries as part of the berry family, you are seriously missing out. Seven other healthy berries include blueberries, raspberries, goji berries, bilberries, acai berries, cranberries, and grapes. Be careful about eating too many fruits per day as they also have a high natural sugar content. About two to three different fruits per day are sufficient.

Leafy Greens and Cruciferous Vegetables

From our listing of vitamin and mineral sources, you will see that leafy, green vegetables are a source of many micro and macronutrients we need.

The cruciferous family of vegetables includes broccoli, cauliflower, and Brussel sprouts are also excellent to include daily. Leafy greens work really well in smoothies, salads, and soups. While cruciferous vegetables like broccoli also work well in salads or as a snack with hummus or a vinaigrette dressing.

Nuts and Seeds

Both nuts and seeds are sources of a wide range of macro and micronutrients, and definitely something to include daily. You could keep them as a snack in a container, sprinkle seeds over salads, and pretty much any other dish, or make homemade seed and nuts power bars for training. The following is a list of the most nutritious nuts in descending order:

- Almonds
- Pistachios
- Walnuts
- Cashews
- Pecans
- Macadamia nuts
- Brazil nuts
- Hazel nuts
- Peanuts

Turmeric and Other Herbs and Spices

Turmeric, of late, has gained major exposure for its distinctive anti-inflammatory properties. When mixed with coconut oil and black pepper, it forms 'golden paste,' recommended as a daily supplement to reduce overall inflammation in the body. It can also be used in many different dishes to elevate the flavor, and probably one of the dishes that contain the most spices with health benefits is curry. When you include turmeric, cumin, garlic, and ginger, you get a powerful intake of some of the healthiest spices available. Various herbs, including parsley, rosemary, and thyme, also have many health benefits. Consider purchasing herbs still on the stalk and store them in a glass of water in the fridge. In this way, they will last up to two weeks, and, as you are cooking, you can snip off some of these green goodness and add it to any dish. Cinnamon is excellent for reducing your blood sugar levels, and can easily be included in your diet by adding a small amount to your tea, cereal, or smoothies.

Beans

Beans are not just great sources of protein; they are also good for our gut health. Unlike other foods, beans are not digested by our gastric juices. Instead, they are broken down by a fermentation process by our gut bacteria (microbiota), which is highly beneficial to the health of these bacteria. Our gut bacteria play a vital role in our body's operations, including our immune system and even our psychological health. Many autoimmune diseases result from imbalanced microbiota, which causes incorrect autoimmune responses. Don't limit yourself in the types of beans you are consuming, as there is a wide range of different types that fit into the bean family. These include:

- Black beans
- Chickpeas (garbanzo beans)
- Kidney beans
- Soybeans (including the immature soybean, edamame)
- Fava beans
- Black-eyed peas

Beans can be added to many different meals, including soups, stews, salads, and curries, or even roasted in the oven as a snack. Hummus is an excellent way to include chickpeas in your diet, and that can be used as a dip or as a spread on sandwiches.

Onions and Garlic

Both onions and garlic are sirtuin activators which keep our metabolism healthy. Garlic also has anti-inflammatory and anti-bacterial properties. It is always best to use fresh garlic when cooking, and if using freshly peeled cloves of garlic, press the clove slightly, and allow it to sit for a few minutes before cooking. This allows the compounds in the garlic to activate fully. Onions also have powerful anti-inflammatory properties that help to reduce the risk of developing chronic disease. Thankfully onions and garlic are a staple of many cooked meals, and in most cases, you don't even taste them after cooking, so there are hardly any meals they don't compliment.

Green Tea

Green tea, a staple beverage in countries around the world, is now known to be a powerful antioxidant and sirtuin activator. There is significant evidence to link low levels of cancer and obesity in Asian countries to green tea consumption. Matcha green tea, which comes in a powder form, is the most effective of the green tea variants, but you can't go wrong by using the teabag form either. Matcha green tea powder can be added to smoothies, and cooled green tea can be made into a refreshing training beverage. There are also green tea supplements, but it is always better to take in the actual source rather than a supplement where possible.

Foods to Eat Weekly

- **Avocado** is a healthy fat source and smart choice before athletic events as it is extremely versatile. Mash it up and serve on whole-wheat toast or puree and add to a salad instead of dressing.

- **Coconut products** like coconut butter, manna, or coconut milk are all great to include weekly. They contain high levels of medium-chain triglycerides, which your body absorbs efficiently to use for energy. These can also be included in smoothies for ease of accessibility. Keep your coconut product intake in moderation as they do contain a high concentration of saturated fats.

- **Ginger** has been used as a plant-based medicine for many years with anti-inflammatory and anti-bacterial properties. It can be taken in through tea, smoothies, or added into stir-fry or curry.

- **Tomatoes** are a powerful source of antioxidants and are also very versatile. They can be taken by juice, salads, or cooked in dishes.

- **Lemon juice** can be used to lift the flavors in any dish and in drinks or smoothies. Lemon juice also contains a high amount of vitamin C, which is great for supporting the immune system and is known to be beneficial in aiding weight loss.

- **Dates** contain sirtuin activators, and are also a healthy replacement to sugary snacks, especially while training. They also work well in nut and seed bars and desserts.

- **Dark chocolate** contains at least 85% cocoa is an excellent way to improve the metabolism. It should always be eaten in moderation, but it is an efficient way to replace sugar-laden milk chocolate bars and cut cravings.

Determining Your Personal Goals

While there is a mass of information available about general guidelines for eating a healthy plant-based diet, it is always vital to ensure that you are planning your nutrition around your personal goals and unique situation.

Every person is different, as is every athlete, and, as such, no single diet will serve every person's needs. Small adjustments will be required to ensure that you are meeting your athletic needs.

The first step is to determine your personal goals, whether for your overall health or athletic performance. When setting goals, be specific. List exactly how much of which criteria you want to increase or decrease, and when you plan to do so.

There are a few aspects that need to be addressed when defining your personal goals.

Fat-Free Mass

Although for the average person working on a simple body mass index may be sufficient to determine progress, we need to delve a bit deeper for athletes. The fat-free mass index (FFMI) accounts for muscle mass, so athletes can measure progress in building muscle. The average male FFMI is about 19, and the average female is around 15. The index is measured in kilograms per square meter (kg/m²). There are several online FFMI calculators, but the general calculation for this index is as follows:

- **Fat free mass = weight (kg) x [1 - (body fat % / 100)]**
- **FFMI = fat free mass (kg) / [height (m)]²**

This macro will be particularly important for athletes who need to build muscle for their disciplines.

Basal Metabolic Rate

This is one of the most common measurements of healthy body weights and is often referred to as basal metabolic index or BMI. This index is a good assessment of your body fat and whether you are overweight, underweight, or within a healthy range for your height, age, and gender. A normal range for an adult is between 18.5 and 24.9. The calculation for the body mass index is as follows:

- **BMI = weight / height^2**
- **Many online calculators will calculate your BMI for you.**

Daily Energy Expenditure

Daily energy expenditure is how much energy we burn, carrying out normal body processes like breathing, digesting food, or circulating blood, as well as exercising. We also burn energy while we sleep and when our body is in a resting state. This index is measured in calories.

Daily energy expenditure varies according to age, gender, activity level, body composition, and even genetics. Again, online calculators are your best bet for getting an easy and relatively accurate energy expenditure number, although it should always be considered that this number is an estimate.

Four factors determine your energy expenditure:

- **Basal metabolic rate (BMR)**
- **The thermic effect of food (TEF)** is the energy we expend in burning food and differs according to your diet's macronutrient composition. If you take in more protein, you will burn more energy than your diet is predominantly carbohydrates.

- **Non-exercise activity thermogenesis (NEAT)** is how much energy we burn during activities that are not seen as structured exercises. This will also differ depending on your job. A waitress, for instance, will have a higher NEAT than an office worker.

- **Thermic effect of activity (TEA)** is how much energy you burn during structured exercise.

The formula for calculating your daily energy expenditure index:

Daily Energy Expenditure = **BMR + TEF + NEAT + TEA**

If you're anything like me, you'll be much happier using one of the many calculators available online instead.

Track Your Macros

To ensure that you can judge your progress, it is vital to track these macros on a regular basis. Use your current indices as a starting point, and then as you move across to a more plant-based diet, regularly (weekly) track those macros to ensure you are on track and adjust your diet accordingly.

Supplements for Plant-Based Diet

As with anything else, the type and amount of supplements you will need will differ from person to person and depending on your athletic needs. As discussed in previous sections, a plant-based diet is lower in specific vitamins than an animal-based diet. These include:

Vitamin B12: the daily recommended intake of B12 is 2.4 mcg per day. Supplements can be in tablet or capsule form, and you can also get B12 injections monthly. Your ability to absorb B12 also decreases as you age, and it is depleted by the use of chronic medications.

Zinc: the daily recommended intake of zinc is between eight and 11 mg for adults. Although you may well get in enough zinc from a varied plant-based diet, supplements are also available in tablet form.

Iodine: vegans are at risk for iodine deficiency, and some studies (Petre, 2019) indicated that vegan iodine levels could be up to 50% lower than those on a meat-based diet. The recommended daily intake for adults is 150 mcg.

- **Vitamin D:** the recommended daily intake is 15 mcg. Deficiencies in this vitamin are not restricted to vegans, as there are very few food sources that contain it at significant enough levels. While, as previously mentioned, sunshine is a good source of vitamin D, there are also negative aspects of spending too much time in the sun. If you use this method to get your intake, always wear sunblock, and protect yourself from skin damage.

- **Vitamin K2:** the general guideline for vitamin K2 intake is 1 mcg per kilogram of weight. Vitamin K2 is available in food sources, but at relatively low levels. You will usually find this vitamin combined in a supplement with vitamin D.

- **Omega-3 fatty acids:** these fatty acids can be divided into essential fatty acids and long-chain fatty acids. Essential fatty acids can only be taken in through the food we eat, and long-chain fatty acids can be manufactured by our bodies. The recommended daily intake of omega-3 fatty acids is between 200 and 300 mg.

Choosing Vegan Supplements

To ensure that you are getting enough of the vitamins and minerals you need, the following is a guide to the supplement levels you should aim for per day:

- 100-200 mg EPA fatty acids
- 300 mg DHA fatty acids
- 300-1000 mcg vitamin B12
- 1000-2000 vitamin
- 150-200 mg magnesium
- 8-12 mg zinc
- 100-150 mcg iodine
- 150-200 mg magnesium
- 50-100 mcg vitamin K2
- 30-50 mcg selenium

It may be useful to visit a dietician or nutritionist to start with so that you can work with a professional to make these decisions and avoid any possible deficiencies or impact on your performance.

When selecting a supplement, don't just accept that it's good for you because the label says it's vegan. Check the ingredients on the nutritional label and see how many added chemicals there are. Try to select a supplement that is as preservative and flavorant-free as possible.

The Recipe

Chapter 2

Breakfast and Smoothies

34	Kiwi-Strawberry Chia Pudding
34	Orange and Strawberry Smoothie
35	Banana and Oat Pancakes
35	Almond Protein Shake
36	Apple and Cinnamon Smoothie
36	Tofu and Spinach Breakfast Scramble
37	Breakfast Burrito
37	Bananas and Peanut Butter Smoothie
38	Vegan Mushroom Omelet
38	Oatmeal Protein Shake
39	Cranberry-Pear Polenta
39	Chocolate Chia Pudding
40	Apple and Walnut Bowl
40	Papaya and Mango Smoothie Cubes
41	Breakfast Skillet

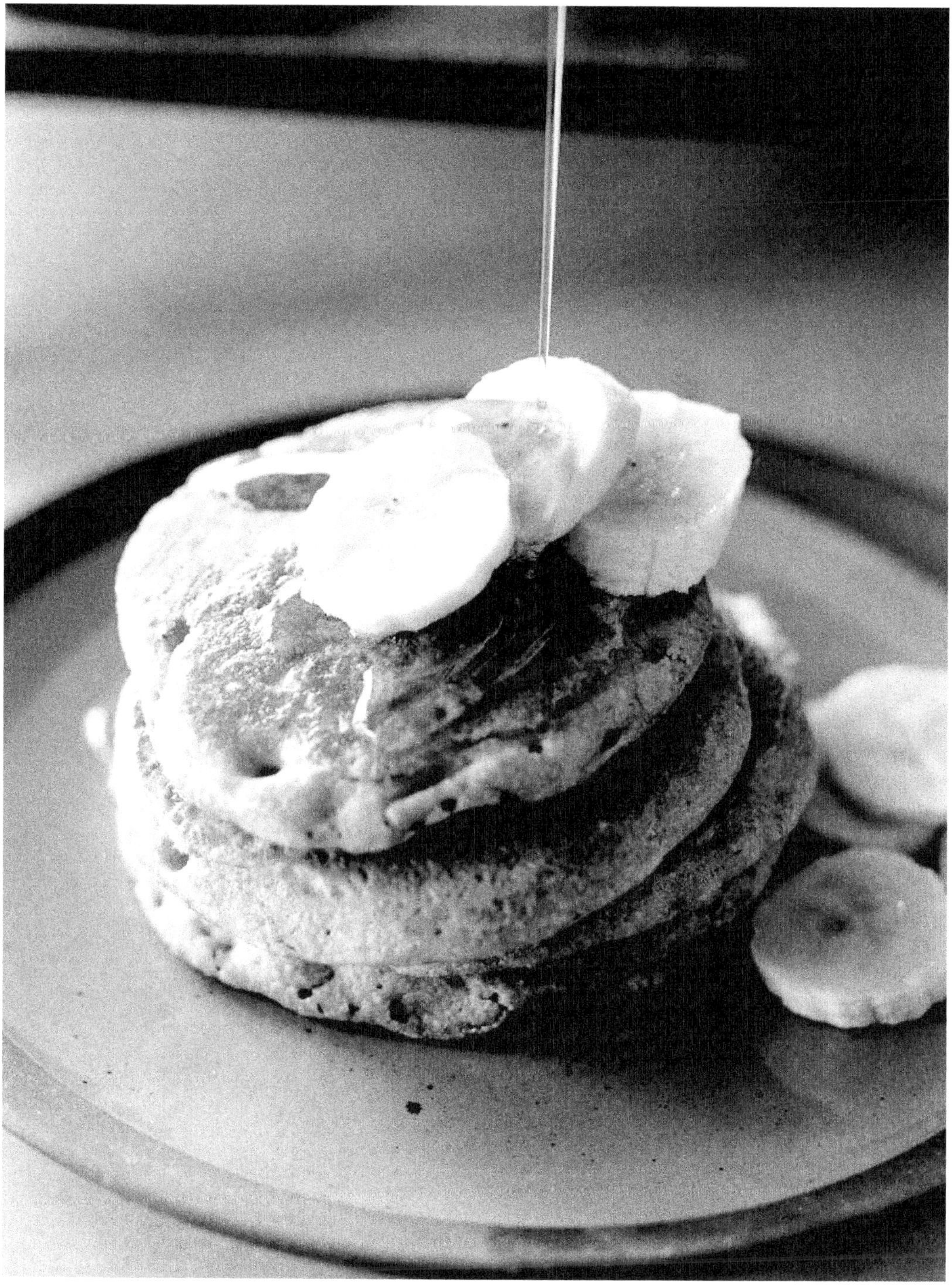

Kiwi-Strawberry Chia Pudding

Prep time: 5 minutes | Cook time: 0 minutes | Serves 2

- 2 cups unsweetened coconut milk, divided
- 3 Medjool dates, pitted
- 1 tablespoon vanilla extract
- ½ cup chia seeds

Toppings:

- 2 kiwis, sliced
- 4 strawberries, sliced
- 2 tablespoons unsweetened coconut shreds
- 2 tablespoons sliced or chopped almonds

1. In a food processor, blend ¾ cup of the unsweetened coconut milk, the dates and vanilla.
2. Pour the blended mix into a large reusable container or Mason jar. Add the remaining 1¼ cups of the unsweetened coconut milk and the chia seeds. Cover the container and shake gently or stir to mix.
3. Store in the refrigerator overnight or for at least 4 hours, until the chia seeds absorb all the milk.
4. When ready to eat, top the pudding with the kiwi, strawberries, coconut, and almonds.
5. Store in the refrigerator for up to 5 days.

Per Serving

calories: 784 | fat: 38.1g | carbs: 79.2g | protein: 27.5g | fiber: 47.8g

Orange and Strawberry Smoothie

Prep time: 5 minutes | Cook time: 0 minutes | Serves 2

- 2 cups unsweetened unsweetened coconut milk
- 10 fresh strawberries
- 1 orange, peeled and parted
- 1 banana
- 3 scoops vanilla flavor vegan protein powder
- 2 ice cubes (optional)

1. Add all the ingredients to a blender.
2. Blend for 2 minutes.
3. Transfer the shake to a large cup.
4. Stir and enjoy.

Per Serving

calories: 288 | fat: 7.6g | carbs: 29.2g | protein: 25.7g | fiber: 4.4g

Banana and Oat Pancakes

Prep time: 5 minutes | Cook time: 18 minutes | Serves 2

- 1½ cups unsweetened plant-based milk
- 1 cup quick oats
- 1 banana
- ½ cup vital wheat gluten
- ½ cup whole wheat flour
- 2 tablespoons maple syrup
- 2 teaspoons vanilla extract
- 1 teaspoon pink Himalayan salt

Optional toppings:

- Sliced bananas
- Pecans
- Hulled hemp seeds
- Maple syrup

1. In a food processor, combine all the ingredients, except for the optional toppings, and mix until smooth.
2. Use a ¼-cup measuring cup to pour ⅙ of the batter into a nonstick skillet over medium heat and cook for 3 minutes. Once the edges of the pancake start to brown and bubble, flip and cook the other side. Repeat with the remaining batter.
3. Serve immediately with the sliced bananas, pecans, hemp seeds or maple syrup.
4. Store the pancakes in the refrigerator in a sealed container for up to 3 days.

Per Serving (3 pancakes)

calories: 547 | fat: 6.2g | carbs: 85.8g | protein: 36.3g | fiber: 11.2g

Almond Protein Shake

Prep time: 5 minutes | Cook time: 0 minutes | Serves 2

- 1½ cups soy milk
- 3 tablespoons almonds
- 1 teaspoon maple syrup
- 1 tablespoon coconut oil
- 2 scoops chocolate or vanilla flavor vegan protein powder
- 2 to 4 ice cubes
- 1 teaspoon cocoa powder (optional)

1. Add all the ingredients to a blender.
2. Blend for 2 minutes.
3. Transfer the shake to a large cup or shaker.
4. Serve immediately.

Per Serving

calories: 341 | fat: 17.1g | carbs: 15.3g | protein: 31.7g | fiber: 1.8g

Apple and Cinnamon Smoothie

Prep time: 5 minutes | Cook time: 0 minutes | Serves 1

- 1 green apple, peeled, cored, and chopped
- 1 cup unsweetened unsweetened coconut milk
- ½ teaspoon cinnamon powder, plus more for topping
- 2 scoops vanilla flavor vegan protein powder
- 3 ice cubes (optional)
- 1 to 2 teaspoons matcha powder (optional)

1. Add all the ingredients to a blender.
2. Blend for 2 minutes.
3. Transfer the shake to a large cup or shaker.
4. Top with some additional cinnamon powder.
5. Serve immediately.

Per Serving

calories: 374 | fat: 10.2g | carbs: 21.8g | protein: 48.6g | fiber: 3.4g

Tofu and Spinach Breakfast Scramble

Prep time: 5 minutes | Cook time: 15 minutes | Serves 2

- 1 (14-ounce / 397-g) package firm or extra-firm tofu
- 4 ounces (113 g) mushrooms, sliced
- ½ bell pepper, diced
- 2 tablespoons nutritional yeast
- 1 tablespoon low-sodium vegetable broth or water
- ½ teaspoon garlic powder
- ½ teaspoon onion powder
- ⅛ teaspoon freshly ground black pepper
- 1 cup fresh spinach

1. Heat a large skillet over medium-low heat.
2. Drain the tofu, then place it in the skillet and mash it down with a fork or mixing spoon. Stir in the mushrooms, bell pepper, nutritional yeast, broth, garlic powder, onion powder, and pepper. Cover and cook for 10 minutes, stirring once after about 5 minutes.
3. Uncover, and stir in the spinach. Cook for an additional 5 minutes before serving.

Per Serving

calories: 231 | fat: 10.2g | carbs: 16.1g | protein: 27.2g | fiber: 7.3g

Breakfast Burrito

Prep time: 5 minutes | Cook time: 15 minutes | Serves 2

- ½ block firm tofu (7 ounces / 198 g)
- 2 medium potatoes, cut into ¼-inch dice
- 1 cup cooked black beans
- 4 ounces (113 g) mushrooms, sliced
- 1 jalapeño, deseeded and diced
- 2 tablespoons low-sodium vegetable broth or water
- 1 tablespoon nutritional yeast
- ½ teaspoon garlic powder
- ½ teaspoon onion powder
- ¼ cup salsa
- 6 corn tortillas

1. Heat a large skillet over medium-low heat.
2. Drain the tofu, then place it in the pan and mash it down with a fork or mixing spoon.
3. Stir the potatoes, black beans, mushrooms, jalapeño, broth, nutritional yeast, garlic powder, and onion powder into the skillet. Reduce the heat to low, cover, and cook for 10 minutes, or until the potatoes can be easily pierced with a fork.
4. Uncover, and stir in the salsa. Cook for 5 minutes, stirring every other minute.
5. Warm the tortillas in a microwave for 15 to 30 seconds or in a warm oven until soft.
6. Remove the pan from the heat, place one-sixth of the filling in the center of each tortilla, and roll the tortillas into burritos before serving.

Per Serving

calories: 536 | fat: 8.2g | carbs: 95.1g | protein: 29.1g | fiber: 21.2g

Bananas and Peanut Butter Smoothie

Prep time: 5 minutes | Cook time: 0 minutes | Serves 1

- 2 bananas
- 1 cup almond milk
- 2 tablespoons peanut butter
- 1 teaspoon cacao powder

1. Cut the bananas into chunks and place in a small freezer-safe container or plastic zip-top bag. Place in the freezer until frozen, at least 30 minutes.
2. To prepare, place all the ingredients in a blender and blend until smooth.
3. Serve immediately.

Per Serving

calories: 501 | fat: 24.2g | carbs: 57.1g | protein: 14.3g | fiber: 11.3g

Vegan Mushroom Omelet

Prep time: 10 minutes | Cook time: 14 to 17 minutes | Makes 2 omelets

- 2 teaspoons olive oil
- 6 spring onions, sliced
- ½ cup mushrooms, sliced
- 1 small pepper, finely chopped
- 2 cloves garlic, minced
- ¾ cup chickpea flour
- 1 teaspoon turmeric
- 1 teaspoon yellow curry powder
- ¼ teaspoon salt
- ½ cup unsweetened plant milk

1. Heat the oil in a sauté pan over medium heat.
2. When warm, add the onions, mushrooms, chili, and garlic.
3. Meanwhile, in a mixing bowl combine the chickpea flour and spices and stir in the plant milk until the texture resembles batter.
4. Once the vegetables are soft, about 5 minutes, pour the batter right over them.
5. Cook oover medium heat for 6 to 8 minutes, until the edges are brown.
6. Using a spatula, flip the omelet.
7. Cook until the outside is lightly brown and cooked thoroughly, 3 to 4 minutes.
8. Serve warm.

Per Serving

calories: 216 | fat: 8.3g | carbs: 27.2g | protein: 10.2g | fiber: 7.0g

Oatmeal Protein Shake

Prep time: 5 minutes | Cook time: 0 minutes | Serves 3

- 1 cup dry oatmeal
- 3 scoops chocolate or vanilla flavor vegan protein powder
- ½ teaspoon cinnamon
- ½ teaspoon maple syrup
- ¼ cup almonds
- 1 cup oat milk
- 2 ice cubes
- 2 tablespoons peanut butter (optional)

1. Add the ingredients to a blender.
2. Blend for 2 minutes.
3. Transfer to a large cup or shaker.
4. Serve immediately.

Per Serving

calories: 299 | fat: 9.1g | carbs: 24.8g | protein: 29.4g | fiber: 4.0g

Cranberry-Pear Polenta

Prep time: 10 minutes | Cook time: 45 minutes | Serves 4

- 5¼ cups water, divided, plus more as needed
- 1½ cups coarse cornmeal
- 3 tablespoons pure maple syrup
- 1 tablespoon molasses
- 1 teaspoon ground cinnamon
- 2 ripe pears, cored and diced
- 1 cup fresh cranberries
- 1 teaspoon chopped fresh rosemary leaves

1. In an 8-quart pot over high heat, bring 5 cups of the water to a simmer.
2. While whisking continuously to avoid clumping, slowly pour in the cornmeal. Cook, stirring often with a heavy spoon, for 30 minutes. The polenta should be thick and creamy.
3. While the polenta cooks, in a saucepan over medium heat, stir together the maple syrup, molasses, the remaining ¼ cup of the water, and the cinnamon until combined. Bring to a simmer. Add the pears and cranberries. Cook for 10 minutes, stirring occasionally, until the pears are tender and start to brown. Remove from the heat. Stir in the rosemary and let the mixture sit for 5 minutes. If it is too thick, add another ¼ cup of water and return to the heat.
4. Top the polenta with the cranberry-pear mixture and serve.

Per Serving

calories: 283 | fat: 2.1g | carbs: 65.3g | protein: 4.4g | fiber: 12.2g

Chocolate Chia Pudding

Prep time: 5 minutes | Cook time: 0 minutes | Serves 2

- ¼ cup chia seeds
- 1 cup unsweetened coconut milk
- 2 tablespoons raw cacao powder
- 1 teaspoon vanilla extract
- 1 teaspoon pure maple syrup

1. In a large bowl, stir together the chia seeds, milk, cacao powder, vanilla, and maple syrup. Divide between 2 (½-pint) covered glass jars or containers. Refrigerate overnight.
2. Stir before serving.

Per Serving

calories: 214 | fat: 10.1g | carbs: 20.2g | protein: 9.1g | fiber: 15.3g

Apple and Walnut Bowl

Prep time: 15 minutes | Cook time: 0 minutes | Serves 4

- 1 green apple, halved, deseeded, and cored
- 3 Honeycrisp apples, halved, deseeded, and cored
- 1 teaspoon freshly squeezed lemon juice
- 5 Medjool dates, pitted
- ½ teaspoon ground cinnamon
- Pinch of ground nutmeg
- 2 tablespoons chia seeds, plus more for serving (optional)
- 1 tablespoon hemp seeds
- ¼ cup chopped walnuts
- Peanut butter, for serving (optional)

1. Finely dice half the green apple and 1 Honeycrisp apple. Store in an airtight container with the lemon juice while you work on next steps.
2. Coarsely chop the remaining apples and the dates. Transfer to a food processor and add the cinnamon and nutmeg. Pulse several times to combine, then process for 2 to 3 minutes to purée. Stir the purée into the reserved diced apples. Stir in the chia seeds (if using), hemp seeds, and walnuts. Refrigerate for at least 1 hour before serving.
3. Serve as is or top with additional chia seeds and peanut butter (if using).

Per Serving

calories: 275 | fat: 8.1g | carbs: 52.2g | protein: 4.3g | fiber: 9.0g

Papaya and Mango Smoothie Cubes

Prep time: 5 minutes | Cook time: 0 minutes | Makes 8 smoothies

- 1 large papaya
- 1 mango
- 2 cups chopped fresh pineapple
- 1 cup raw cauliflower florets
- 2 large navel oranges, peeled and halved
- 1 large orange bell pepper, stemmed, deseeded, and coarsely chopped

1. Halve the papaya and mango, remove the pits, and scoop their soft flesh into a high-speed blender.
2. Add the pineapple, cauliflower, oranges, and bell pepper. Blend until smooth.
3. Evenly divide the purée between 2 (16-compartment) ice cube trays and place on a level surface in the freezer. Freeze for at least 8 hours.
4. The cubes can be left in the ice cube trays until use or transferred to a freezer bag. The frozen cubes are good for about 3 weeks in a standard freezer, or up to 6 months in a chest freezer.

Per Serving (1 smoothie)

calories: 97 | fat: 0.9g | carbs: 24.1g | protein: 2.3g | fiber: 4.1g

Breakfast Skillet

Prep time: 15 minutes | Cook time: 40 minutes | Serves 2

For the Potatoes:

- 2 tablespoons low-sodium vegetable broth
- ¼ teaspoon garlic powder
- ¼ teaspoon freshly ground black pepper
- ⅛ teaspoon pink Himalayan salt
- 3 yellow potatoes, chopped

For the Skillet:

- 1 tablespoon paprika
- ¼ teaspoon freshly ground black pepper
- ⅛ teaspoon pink Himalayan salt
- ⅛ teaspoon turmeric
- 3 cups baby spinach
- ½ block firm tofu, cubed
- 6 slices tempeh, chopped
- ¼ cup low-sodium vegetable broth
- 1 yellow onion, chopped
- 1 red bell pepper, diced
- 3 garlic cloves, minced

1. Preheat the oven to 400ºF (205ºC). Line a baking sheet with parchment paper or a silicone liner.
2. In a large bowl, mix the broth, garlic powder, pepper, and salt. Add the potatoes and mix well.
3. Spread the potatoes on the prepared baking sheet and bake for 30 minutes, or until soft and browned on the edges.
4. In a small bowl, mix the paprika, black pepper, salt, and turmeric.
5. In a large nonstick skillet over medium heat, combine the spinach, tofu, tempeh, broth, onion, bell pepper, and garlic. Stir in the seasoning mix. Cover the skillet and cook for 5 minutes. Add the baked potatoes and cook, stirring frequently, for another 5 minutes.
6. Serve immediately or store in the refrigerator in a sealed container for up to 3 days.

Per Serving

calories: 434 | fat: 8.3g | carbs: 68.1g | protein: 27.4g | fiber: 14.2g

Chapter 3

Pre-Training Meals

44	Mango and Orange Smoothie
44	Banana and Blueberry Smoothie
45	Chocolate-Banana Smoothie Bowl
45	Vanilla Banana Smoothie
46	Cinnamon-Vanilla French Toast

Pre-Training Meals | 43

Mango and Orange Smoothie

Prep time: 5 minutes | Cook time: 0 minutes | Serves 2

- 1 orange, peeled and parted
- 1 cup fresh mango chunks
- 1 banana
- ½ cup blueberries
- 2 scoops chocolate or vanilla flavor vegan protein powder
- 1 tablespoon hemp seeds
- 1 teaspoon guarana (optional)
- 6 ice cubes

1. Add all the ingredients to a blender.
2. Blend for 2 minutes.
3. Transfer the shake to a large cup or shaker.
4. Serve immediately.

Per Serving

calories: 351 | fat: 6.8g | carbs: 44.5g | protein: 28.1g | fiber: 5.9g

Banana and Blueberry Smoothie

Prep time: 5 minutes | Cook time: 0 minutes | Serves 1

- 1 medium banana
- ½ cup frozen wild blueberries
- ½ cup frozen mango chunks
- 1 cup plain coconut water

1. Cut the banana into chunks and place in a small freezer-safe container or plastic zip-top bag along with the blueberries and mango. Keep frozen until ready to use.
2. To prepare, place all ingredients in a blender and blend until smooth. Serve immediately.

Per Serving

calories: 254 | fat: 1.2g | carbs: 59.1g | protein: 2.3g | fiber: 7.1g

Chocolate-Banana Smoothie Bowl

Prep time: 5 minutes | Cook time: 0 minutes | Serves 1

Smoothie Bowl:

- 1 frozen banana, 4 slices reserved for topping
- ½ cup almond milk
- 1 tablespoon almond butter
- 1 tablespoon cocoa powder
- 1 tablespoon maple syrup
- 1 cup spinach

Toppings:

- 4 banana slices (from above)
- 1 strawberry, sliced
- 2 tablespoons dairy-free chocolate chips
- 2 tablespoons raw shelled hempseed

1. Add all the ingredients for smoothie bowl to a blender and blend until smooth.
2. Pour into a bowl and serve garnished with the toppings.

Per Serving

calories: 479 | fat: 25.3g | carbs: 63.7g | protein: 7.9g | fiber: 7.8g

Vanilla Banana Smoothie

Prep time: 5 minutes | Cook time: 0 minutes | Serves 1

- 1 frozen banana, sliced
- 1 cup vanilla almond milk
- ¼ cup old-fashioned oats
- ¼ cup raisins
- 1 tablespoon flaxseed meal
- ¼ teaspoon cinnamon
- 3 tablespoons vanilla protein powder

1. Add all the ingredients to a blender and blend until very smooth.
2. Serve immediately.

Per Serving

calories: 706 | fat: 21.2g | carbs: 102.8g | protein: 33.6g | fiber: 14.1g

Cinnamon-Vanilla French Toast

Prep time: 5 minutes | Cook time: 10 minutes | Serves 2

- 1 cup unsweetened plant-based milk
- ¾ cup firm tofu
- ½ teaspoon vanilla extract
- ½ teaspoon ground cinnamon
- ¼ teaspoon ground flaxseed
- 4 slices thick whole wheat bread

1. In a blender, blend the milk, tofu, vanilla, cinnamon, and flaxseed until smooth.
2. Pour the mixture into a wide bowl. Dip the bread slices into the mixture until evenly coated on both sides.
3. In a medium nonstick pan over medium heat, cook the bread slices for 10 minutes, flipping when the bottom is light brown. Flip again, if needed.
4. Serve warm.

Per Serving

calories: 643 | fat: 20.1g | carbs:92.2g protein: 31.4g | fiber: 14.2g

Chapter 4

Midday Meals

49	Golden Tofu Brown Rice Bowl
49	Citrus Kale Salad
50	Quinoa Bowl with Basil Pesto
50	Sushi Bowl with Veggies
51	Mango Quinoa Bowl with Tempeh
51	Tofu Club Wrap
52	Teriyaki Tempeh Lettuce Wraps
52	Pesto Pasta Salad
53	Stuffed Avocado
53	Couscous Salad with Chickpeas
54	Stacked Portobello Burgers
55	Cauliflower Rice with Satay Tempeh
56	Sesame Tempeh in Soy Sauce
56	Sweet Potato and Broccoli Bowl
57	Classic Chana Masala
58	Farro Bowl with Kidney Beans
58	Mac 'N' Mince
59	Smoked Tofu and Black Beans Bowl
60	Soba Noodles with Tempeh

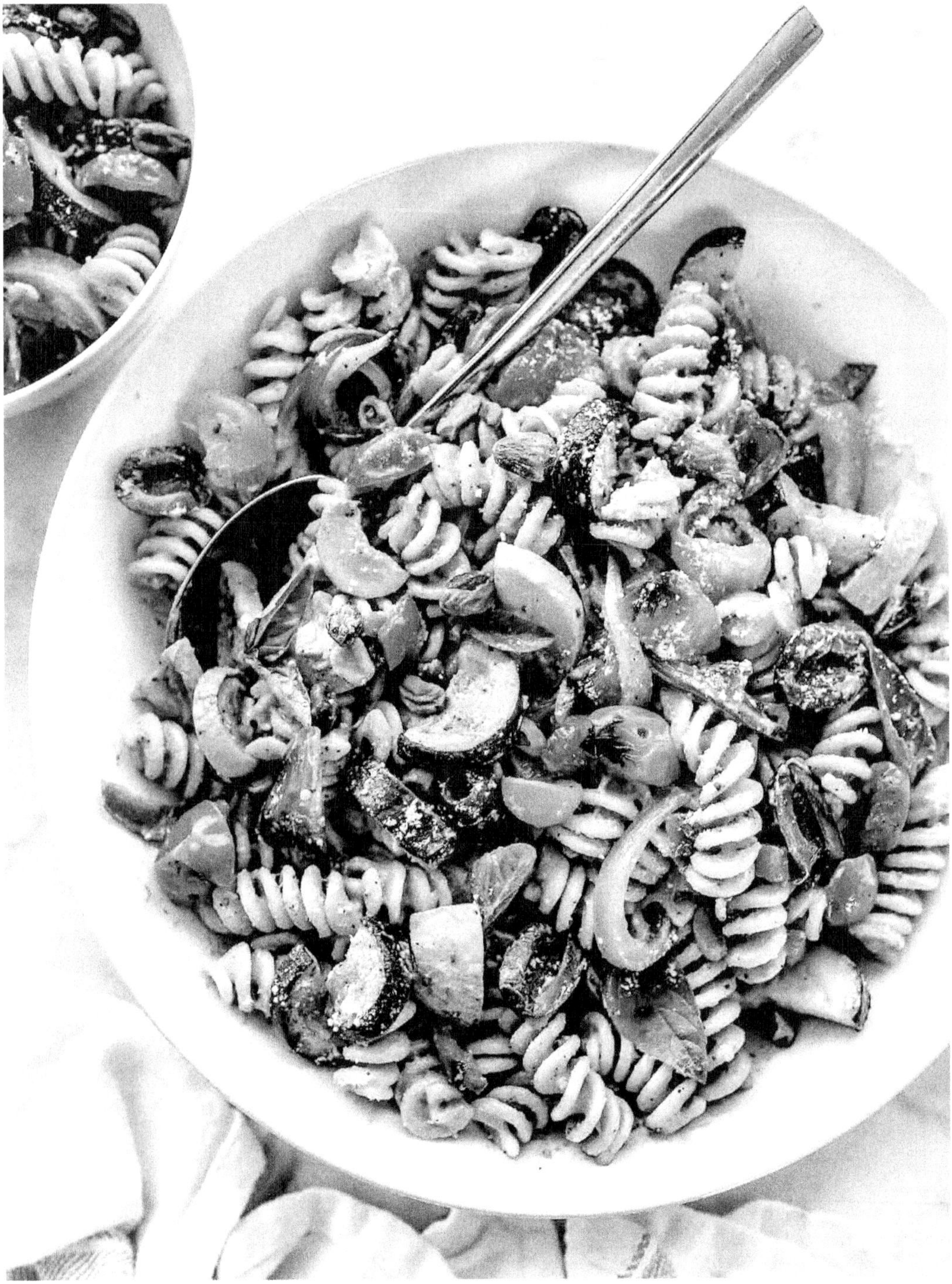

Golden Tofu Brown Rice Bowl

Prep time: 15 minutes | Cook time: 5 minutes | Serves 2

- 1 cup firm tofu, cubed
- 2 tablespoons coconut oil
- 6 cups cooked brown rice
- 1 cup shelled edamame, steamed
- 1 large carrot, peeled
- ½ cucumber, sliced
- 1 radish, sliced
- ¼ cup pickled red cabbage (optional)
- Roasted sesame seeds (optional)

Soy Hoisin Sauce:

- 3 tablespoons hoisin sauce
- 1 teaspoon sriracha
- ¼ cup soy sauce
- 1 lime, squeezed

1. Put all the ingredients for soy hoisin sauce into a small bowl and stir well. Set the sauce aside.
2. Take a large skillet, put it on medium heat and add the coconut oil.
3. Stir fry the tofu for about 5 minutes until brown before stirring in the hoisin sauce.
4. Serve the cooked rice with the tofu and sauce in a bowl.
5. Top the dish with the steamed edamame, carrot, cucumber and raw radish.
6. Add the optional roasted sesame seeds and pickled red cabbage.
7. Serve and enjoy or store the fresh and cooked ingredients in multiple-compartment containers.

Per Serving

calories: 548 | fat: 22.5g | carbs: 63.4g | protein: 23.4g | fiber: 9.4g

Citrus Kale Salad

Prep time: 5 minutes | Cook time: 0 minutes | Serves 2

- 4 cups chopped kale
- 2 tablespoons freshly squeezed lemon juice
- ⅛ teaspoon pink Himalayan salt
- 1 cup cooked wild rice
- 1 cup cooked quinoa
- 1 small tomato, chopped
- 1 small avocado, pitted, peeled, and chopped

1. In a large bowl, massage the kale with the lemon juice and salt for a few minutes, or until the kale softens.
2. Add the rice, quinoa, tomato, and avocado to the bowl and mix well.
3. Serve immediately or store in the refrigerator for up to 3 days.

Per Serving

calories: 721 | fat: 20.2g | carbs: 123.1g | protein: 27.2g | fiber: 27.9g

Quinoa Bowl with Basil Pesto

Prep time: 10 minutes | Cook time: 10 minutes | Serves 1

- 1 teaspoon olive oil, or 1 tablespoon low-sodium vegetable broth or water
- 1 cup chopped onion
- 1 garlic clove, minced
- 1 cup chopped zucchini
- Pinch of sea salt
- 1 tomato, chopped
- 2 tablespoons chopped sun-dried tomatoes
- 2 to 3 tablespoons basil pesto
- 1 cup chopped spinach
- 2 cups cooked quinoa

1. Heat the oil in a large skillet on medium-high, then sauté the onion for about 5 minutes. Add the garlic when the onion has softened, then add the zucchini and salt.
2. Once the zucchini is somewhat soft, about 5 minutes, turn off the heat and add the fresh and sun-dried tomatoes. Mix to combine, then toss in the pesto. Toss the vegetables to coat them.
3. Layer the spinach, then quinoa, then the zucchini mixture on a plate and serve.

Per Serving

calories: 536 | fat: 22.8g | carbs: 9.2g | protein: 20.2g | fiber: 14.1g

Sushi Bowl with Veggies

Prep time: 15 minutes | Cook time: 0 minutes | Serves 1

- 1 cup cooked brown rice
- 1 small avocado, pitted, peeled, and cut into strips
- ½ cup shelled edamame
- ½ cup thinly sliced carrots
- ½ cucumber, cut into thin strips
- 1 scallion, chopped
- ½ nori sheet, cut into thin strips

Optional Toppings:

- Low-sodium soy sauce
- Pickled ginger
- Black sesame seeds
- Wasabi

1. Put the rice in a serving bowl and layer on the avocado, edamame, carrots, cucumber, scallion, and nori. Add your toppings of choice (if using).
2. Serve immediately or store in a reusable container in the refrigerator for up to 5 days.

Per Serving

calories: 665 | fat: 32.1g | carbs: 80.8g | protein: 21.3g | fiber: 20.9g

Mango Quinoa Bowl with Tempeh

Prep time: 5 minutes | Cook time: 15 minutes | Serves 4

- 1 cup fresh mango cubes
- 1 (14-ounce / 397-g) pack tempeh, sliced
- 1 cup peanut butter
- 1 cup cooked black beans
- 2 cups cooked quinoa

Optional Toppings:
- Chili flakes
- Shredded coconut

1. Blend the mango into a smooth purée using a blender or food processor, and set it aside.
2. Add the tempeh slices and the peanut butter to an airtight container. Close the lid and shake well until the tempeh slices are evenly covered with the peanut butter.
3. Preheat the oven to 375ºF (190ºC) and line a baking sheet with parchment paper.
4. Transfer the tempeh slices onto the baking sheet and bake for about 15 minutes or until the tempeh is browned and crispy.
5. Divide the black beans, quinoa, mango purée and tempeh slices between two bowls, serve with the optional toppings and enjoy.

Per Serving

calories: 733 | fat: 42.3g | carbs: 39.2g | protein: 46.4g | fiber: 17.3g

Tofu Club Wrap

Prep time: 10 minutes | Cook time: 3 to 5 minutes | Serves 1

- ¼ block firm tofu, sliced
- 3 slices tempeh
- 1 large gluten-free tortilla wrap
- 1 tablespoon vegan mayonnaise
- 1 small avocado, pitted, peeled, and chopped
- 1 romaine lettuce leaf, chopped
- 1 small tomato, sliced
- ¼ small red onion, sliced
- ⅛ teaspoon freshly ground black pepper

1. Preheat a nonstick pan over medium heat. Place the tofu slices and tempeh in the pan and cook for 3 to 5 minutes, until both sides are lightly browned.
2. Place the tortilla on a plate and spread with the mayo. Layer on the avocado, lettuce, tomato, and onion. Top with the tofu and tempeh and sprinkle with the pepper. Wrap the tortilla and serve.

Per Serving

calories: 577 | fat: 29.8g | carbs: 60.2g | protein: 23.3g | fiber: 15.1g

Teriyaki Tempeh Lettuce Wraps

Prep time: 10 minutes | Cook time: 15 minutes | Serves 4

- 1 (14-ounce / 397-g) pack tempeh
- ¼ cup teriyaki sauce
- 1 small red onion, minced
- 1 cup julienned carrots
- 4 large lettuce leaves

Optional Toppings:

- Chili flakes
- Lime juice
- Peanut butter

1. Cut the tempeh into small cubes, put them into an airtight container and add the teriyaki sauce.
2. Close the airtight container, shake well and put it in the fridge, allowing the tempeh to marinate for at least 1 hour, up to 12 hours.
3. Preheat the oven to 375ºF (190ºC) and line a baking sheet with parchment paper.
4. Transfer the tempeh cubes onto the baking sheet and bake for about 15 minutes or until the tempeh is browned and crispy.
5. Lay out 4 large lettuce leaves, add a quarter of the tempeh to each leaf, and top it with the minced red onion and julienned carrots.
6. Serve with the optional toppings.

Per Serving

calories: 227 | fat: 9.7g | carbs: 8.2g | protein: 24.3g | fiber: 6.5g

Pesto Pasta Salad

Prep time: 5 minutes | Cook time: 0 minutes | Serves 4

- 2½ cups fresh basil
- 2 cups fresh spinach
- 1 cup chopped fresh kale
- 4 cloves garlic
- 4 tablespoons freshly squeezed lemon juice
- ¼ teaspoon salt
- ⅛ teaspoon freshly ground black pepper
- 1 cup sunflower seeds
- 8 ounces (227 g) cooked chickpea-based pasta or whole wheat pasta
- 1½ cups chopped fresh tomatoes

1. In a food processor, combine the basil, spinach, kale, garlic, lemon juice, salt, and pepper, and pulse until lightly blended. Add the sunflower seeds and mix until blended well.
2. In a large bowl, combine the pesto sauce with the cooked pasta and mix well. Top with the tomatoes and serve.

Per Serving

calories: 417 | fat: 20.2g | carbs: 47.9g | protein: 23.2g | fiber: 14.1g

Stuffed Avocado

Prep time: 5 minutes | Cook time: 0 minutes | Serves 1

- ½ block firm tofu, cubed
- ¼ cup freshly squeezed lemon juice
- 2 tablespoons unsweetened plant-based milk
- 1 tablespoon apple cider vinegar
- ½ tablespoon dried oregano
- 1 teaspoon nutritional yeast
- ¼ teaspoon pink Himalayan salt
- Pinch of freshly ground black pepper
- 1 large avocado
- 4 cherry tomatoes, diced
- ½ small red onion, diced
- ½ small cucumber, diced
- 1 tablespoon sliced black olives

1. In a reusable container with a lid, combine the tofu, lemon juice, milk, vinegar, oregano, nutritional yeast, salt, and pepper. Cover and gently shake to mix. Marinate in the refrigerator for at least 1 hour.
2. Cut the avocado in half, remove the pit, and stuff both halves with the tomatoes, onion, cucumber, olives, and tofu feta.
3. Serve immediately.

Per Serving

calories: 604 | fat: 41.1g | carbs: 43.2 g | protein: 29.2g | fiber: 21.1g

Couscous Salad with Chickpeas

Prep time: 10 minutes | Cook time: 5 minutes | Serves 1

- 1½ cups water
- 1 cup couscous
- ½ cup cooked chickpeas
- ½ small red bell pepper, chopped
- 1 small red onion, diced
- ½ cucumber, chopped
- 1 small tomato, chopped
- 1 scallion, chopped
- 1 tablespoon balsamic vinegar
- ⅛ teaspoon pink Himalayan salt
- ⅛ teaspoon freshly ground black pepper

1. In a nonstick pot over medium-high heat, bring the water to a boil. Add the couscous. Turn off the heat, stir the couscous, and cover. Let it sit for 5 minutes, until the couscous has fully absorbed the water and is soft.
2. Transfer the couscous to a bowl. Stir in the chickpeas, bell pepper, onion, cucumber, tomato, scallion, vinegar, salt, and black pepper.
3. Serve immediately or store in a reusable container in the refrigerator for up to 7 days.

Per Serving

calories: 821 | fat: 3.2g | carbs: 170.1g | protein: 29.3g | fiber: 16.8g

Stacked Portobello Burgers

Prep time: 20 minutes | Cook time: 20 to 22 minutes | Serves 2

- 1 block firm tofu, drained (8 ounces / 227 g)
- 1 tablespoon extra-virgin olive oil
- 4 large portobello mushroom caps, stems removed
- 1 tablespoon taco seasoning
- ½ teaspoon paprika
- ¼ teaspoon chili powder
- Salt, to taste
- 1 large onion, diced
- ½ green bell pepper, deseeded and diced
- ½ red bell pepper, deseeded and diced
- 3 cups fresh spinach, rinsed and dried
- 2 whole wheat vegan buns
- 4 tablespoons store-bought hummus
- ¼ cup salsa

1. Cut the tofu into 4 large slices and set aside.
2. Heat the olive oil in a large skillet over medium-high heat.
3. Add the mushroom caps and flip them over after 4 minutes of cooking.
4. Sprinkle the caps with the taco seasoning, paprika, chili powder, and salt.
5. Flip again after 4 minutes, allowing them to cook until they have halved in size. Remove the caps from the skillet and set aside.
6. Add the tofu slices to the previously used skillet and cook them on both sides until slightly brown. Set aside.
7. Add the diced onions and bell peppers to the skillet. Stir frequently and cook the vegetables until browned, for 10 to 12 minutes.
8. Turn the heat down to low and add the mushrooms back to the skillet, and reheat for 2 more minutes.
9. Spread hummus on one side of each bun, and the salsa on the other half.
10. Top the hummus with a handful of spinach and serve with two mushroom caps, tofu squares, and top with a heaping scoop of vegetables with more salt.
11. Serve immediately.

Per Serving

calories: 422 | fat: 16.2g | carbs: 48.8g | protein: 20.6g | fiber: 9.9g

Cauliflower Rice with Satay Tempeh

Prep time: 10 minutes | Cook time: 15 minutes | Serves 4

Sauce:

- ¼ cup water
- 4 tablespoons peanut butter
- 3 tablespoons low-sodium soy sauce
- 2 tablespoons coconut sugar
- 1 garlic clove, minced
- ½-inch ginger, minced
- 2 teaspoons rice vinegar
- 1 teaspoon red pepper flakes

Main Ingredients:

- 4 tablespoons olive oil, divided
- 2 (8-ounce / 227-g) packages tempeh, drained
- 2 cups cauliflower rice
- 1 cup diced purple cabbage
- 1 tablespoon sesame oil
- 1 teaspoon agave nectar

1. Take a large bowl, combine all the ingredients for the sauce, and then whisk until the mixture is smooth and any lumps have dissolved.
2. Cut the tempeh into ½-inch cubes and put them into the sauce, stirring to make sure the cubes get coated thoroughly.
3. Place the bowl in the refrigerator to marinate the tempeh for up to 3 hours.
4. Before the tempeh is done marinating, preheat the oven to 400ºF (205ºC).
5. Spread the tempeh out in a single layer on a baking sheet lined with parchment paper.
6. Bake the marinated cubes for about 15 minutes, until browned and crisp.
7. Heat the cauliflower rice in a saucepan with 2 tablespoons of olive oil over medium heat until it is warm.
8. Rinse the large bowl with water, and then mix the cabbage, sesame oil and agave together.
9. Serve a scoop of the cauliflower rice topped with the marinated cabbage and cooked tempeh on a plate.

Per Serving

calories: 532 | fat: 33.2g | carbs:31.8g | protein: 27.7g | fiber: 14.9g

Sesame Tempeh in Soy Sauce

Prep time: 5 minutes | Cook time: 20 minutes | Serves 4

- 1 (14-ounce / 397-g) pack tempeh
- ¼ cup low-sodium soy sauce
- 2 medium onions, minced
- 3 cloves garlic, minced
- ½ cup water

Optional Toppings:

- Sauerkraut
- Roasted sesame seeds
- Shredded coconut

1. Cut the tempeh into thin slices, put them into an airtight container and add the soy sauce.
2. Close the airtight container, shake well and put it in the fridge, allowing the tempeh to marinate for at least 1 hour, or up to 12 hours.
3. Put a nonstick deep frying pan over medium-high heat and add the minced onions, minced garlic and the water.
4. Stir continuously until everything is cooked, then add the tempeh slices.
5. Let it cook for about 20 minutes while stirring occasionally.
6. Turn the heat off, leave to cool down for a minute and drain the excess water if necessary.
7. Divide between 2 plates, garnish with the optional toppings and enjoy!

Per Serving

calories: 212 | fat: 9.7g | carbs: 4.3g | protein: 24.1g | fiber: 6.7g

Sweet Potato and Broccoli Bowl

Prep time: 5 minutes | Cook time: 18 minutes | Serves 2

- 4 sweet potatoes, cubed
- 1 (7-ounce / 198-g) pack smoked tofu, cubed
- 2 cups broccoli florets
- ¼ cup teriyaki sauce
- ¼ cup peanut butter
- ½ cup water

Optional Toppings:

- Chili flakes
- Shredded coconut
- Roasted sesame seeds

1. Cook the sweet potato cubes, covered with water, in a medium pot over medium-high heat for about 10 minutes.
2. Add the broccoli florets, and cook for another 3 minutes.

3. Take the pot off the heat, drain the excess water from the broccoli and sweet potatoes and set aside.
4. Put a nonstick deep frying pan over medium-high heat and add the teriyaki sauce, the water and tofu cubes.
5. Keep stirring continuously until everything is cooked, then add the broccoli florets and sweet potato cubes to the frying pan.
6. Cook for about 5 minutes while stirring occasionally.
7. Turn the heat off, leave to cool down for a minute, then drain the excess water.
8. Divide between 2 plates, drizzle half of the peanut butter on top of each plate with the optional toppings and enjoy!

Per Serving

calories: 550 | fat: 24.1g | carbs:51.2g | protein: 32.3g | fiber: 13.3g

Classic Chana Masala

Prep time: 5 minutes | Cook time: 30 minutes | Serves 2

- 1 cup fresh tomato cubes
- 2 medium onions, minced
- ¼ cup water
- 2 cups cooked chickpeas
- 2 tablespoons curry spices

Optional Toppings:

- Fresh chili slices
- Lime juice
- Shredded coconut

1. Put a large pot over medium heat, then add the tomato cubes, onions, and the water.
2. Cook for 5 minutes, stirring occasionally, until everything is cooked, then add the curry spices and stir thoroughly.
3. Add the chickpeas, and stir thoroughly to make sure that everything is well mixed.
4. Cook for 5 more minutes, stirring occasionally, then lower the heat to a simmer.
5. Let the curry simmer for about 20 minutes while stirring occasionally.
6. Turn the heat off and let the curry cool down for a minute.
7. Divide curry between 2 bowls and serve garnished with the optional toppings.

Per Serving

calories: 402 | fat: 6.3g | carbs: 65.6g | protein: 21.1g | fiber: 20.4g

Farro Bowl with Kidney Beans

Prep time: 15 minutes | Cook time: 30 minutes | Serves 4

- 1½ cups dried farro
- 4 cups water, plus 1 tablespoon and more as needed
- 1 onion, diced
- 5 garlic cloves, minced
- 2 roasted red peppers
- 1 (15-ounce / 425-g) can diced tomatoes
- 1 cup low-sodium vegetable broth
- 1 tablespoon tamari
- 1 tablespoon dried parsley
- 1 teaspoon paprika
- ½ teaspoon dried thyme
- ½ teaspoon cayenne pepper
- 1 (15-ounce / 425-g) can red kidney beans, drained and rinsed

1. In an 8-quart pot over high heat, combine the farro and 4 cups of water. Bring to a boil. Reduce the heat to medium-low, cover the pot, and cook for 25 minutes. Add more water, ½ cup at a time, if the farro looks too dry.
2. While the farro cooks, in a sauté pan or skillet over medium-high heat, cook the onion and garlic for 5 minutes, adding water, 1 tablespoon at a time, to prevent burning. The onion should be browned but not burned.
3. Transfer to a blender and add the roasted red peppers, tomatoes with their juices, low-sodium vegetable broth, tamari, parsley, paprika, thyme, and cayenne pepper. Purée until smooth.
4. Stir the sauce and kidney beans into the cooked farro. Cook over medium-low heat, stirring, until the sauce starts to bubble. Turn off the heat, cover the pot, and let sit for 10 minutes before serving.

Per Serving

calories: 413 | fat: 2.2g | carbs: 85.1g | protein: 19.2g | fiber: 17.3g

Mac 'N' Mince

Prep time: 5 minutes | Cook time: 11 to 13 minutes | Serves 4

- 2 cups whole wheat macaroni
- 1 (7-ounce / 198-g) pack textured soya mince
- ½ cup tahini
- ¼ cup nutritional yeast
- 2 tablespoons lemon garlic pepper seasoning
- ½ cup water, divided
- 2 tablespoons turmeric

Optional Toppings:

- Sun-dried tomatoes
- Crispy onions

1. In a large pot, bring the water to a boil. Add the macaroni and return to a boil. Cook, uncovered, for 6 to 8 minutes or until tender, stirring frequently. Rinse and drain. Set aside.
2. Put a nonstick deep frying pan over medium high heat and add the soya mince with the ¼ cup of water.
3. Stir fry the soya mince for 5 minutes, until it is cooked and most of the water has evaporated.
4. Add the tahini, ¼ cup of water, nutritional yeast, lemon garlic pepper seasoning and turmeric to the soya mince.
5. Cook a little longer, stirring continuously, until everything is well combined.
6. Add the cooked macaroni to the pan with soya mince and stir thoroughly until the mac 'n' mince is mixed well.
7. Divide the mac 'n' mince between two plates, serve with the optional toppings and enjoy!

Per Serving

calories: 455 | fat: 20.1g | carbs:42.2g | protein: 25.2g | fiber: 9.8g

Smoked Tofu and Black Beans Bowl

Prep time: 10 minutes | Cook time: 10 minutes | Serves 2

- 1 (7-ounce / 198-g) pack smoked tofu, cubed
- 1 small hass avocado, peeled and stoned
- 1 cup cooked black beans
- 2 cups cooked sweet corn
- ¼ cup lemon juice

Optional Toppings:

- Jalapeño slices
- Fresh cilantro
- Red onion

1. Preheat the oven to 350ºF (180ºC) and line a baking sheet with parchment paper.
2. Put the tofu cubes on the baking sheet and bake for 10 minutes or until the tofu is slightly browned and dry.
3. Take the tofu cubes out of the oven and let them cool down for about 5 minutes.
4. Cut one half of the peeled avocado into cubes and the other half into slices.
5. Toss the tofu cubes, black beans, avocado cubes, and corn in a large salad bowl and stir well using a spatula until everything is evenly mixed.
6. Divide between two bowls if necessary, then drizzle 2 tablespoons of lemon juice on top of each bowl, garnish with the avocado slices, serve with the optional toppings and enjoy!

Per Serving

calories: 423 | fat: 17.7g | carbs:39.1g | protein: 26.8g | fiber: 12.9g

Soba Noodles with Tempeh

Prep time: 10 minutes | Cook time: 13 to 20 minutes | Serves 4

For the Sauce:

- 6 tablespoons tahini paste
- ¼ cup water
- 4 tablespoons freshly squeezed lemon juice
- 4-inch fresh ginger root, minced
- 4 teaspoons apple cider vinegar
- 4 teaspoons maple syrup
- 4 teaspoons red pepper flakes
- 4 teaspoons low-sodium soy sauce
- ½ teaspoon pink Himalayan salt
- ½ teaspoon freshly ground black pepper

For the Noodles:

- 12 slices tempeh
- 2 tablespoons water
- ¼ teaspoon freshly ground black pepper
- ¼ teaspoon pink Himalayan salt
- 8 ounces (227 g) cooked soba noodles
- 1 red bell pepper, chopped
- 1 carrot, chopped
- 1 cup snow peas
- 1 cup sliced mushrooms
- Scallions, chopped, for topping (optional)
- Sesame seeds, for topping (optional)

1. In a bowl, combine all the ingredients for the sauce and mix well.
2. In a large nonstick pan over medium heat, warm the tempeh with the water, pepper, and salt for 3 to 5 minutes, continuously flipping the tempeh. Add the sauce, noodles, bell pepper, carrot, snow peas, and mushrooms and stir together. Reduce the heat to medium, cover the pan with a lid, and cook, stirring frequently, for 10 to 15 minutes.
3. Serve immediately, garnished with scallions and sesame seeds (if using), or store in a reusable container in the refrigerator for up to 5 days.

Per Serving

calories: 445 | fat: 16.1g | carbs:62.9g protein: 18.8g | fiber: 6.2g

Chapter 5

Post-Training Meals

63	Chickpea and Spinach Salad
63	Simple Chickpea Salad Sandwich
64	Black Bean and Avocado Salad
64	5-Bean Chili
65	Sumptuous Buddha Bowl
66	Air-Fried Seitan
66	Zoodles with Crunchy Sesame Tofu
67	Asian Noodles with Nutty Tofu Crisp
68	Kale Slaw Tacos
69	Tacos with Tempeh and Baked Cauliflower
70	Spicy Soba Noodles with Peanut Sauce
71	Brown Rice and Black Bean Burritos
72	Spiced Veggie Fajitas
72	Pasta with Ricotta Red Sauce
73	Crispy Baked Tempeh

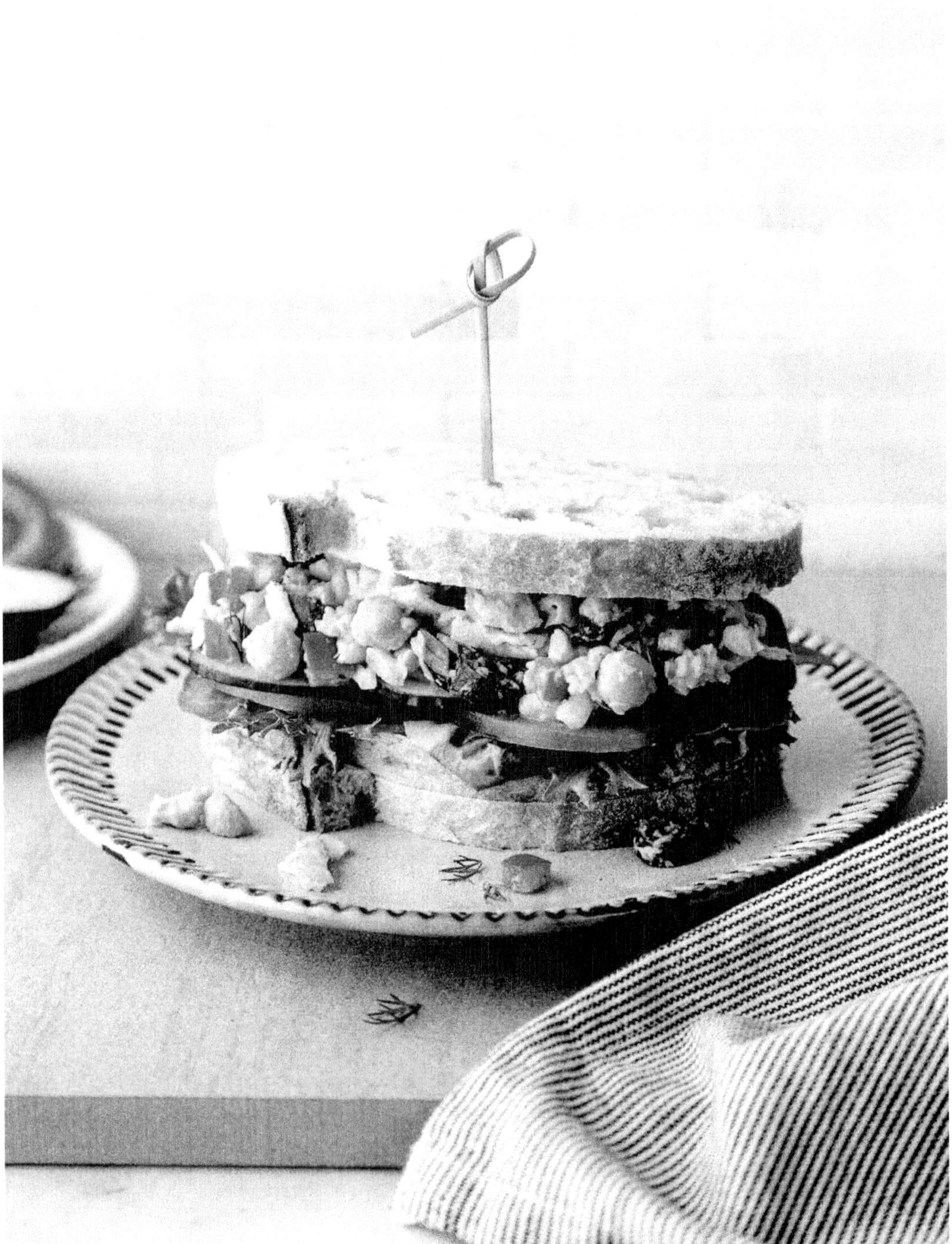

Chickpea and Spinach Salad

Prep time: 10 minutes | Cook time: 0 minutes | Serves 1

- 3 cups roughly chopped baby spinach
- 2 cups cooked chickpeas
- 1 cup chopped mushrooms
- 1 tomato, chopped
- 1 avocado, peeled, pitted, and chopped
- ⅛ teaspoon pink Himalayan salt
- ⅛ teaspoon freshly ground black pepper
- Juice of 1 large lemon
- 1 tablespoon sunflower seeds, for topping (optional)
- 1 teaspoon hulled hemp seeds, for topping (optional)

1. In a large bowl, combine the spinach, chickpeas, mushrooms, tomato, and avocado. Add the salt, pepper, and lemon juice. Mix thoroughly so all the flavors combine and the avocado is mixed in well.
2. Top with the seeds (if using). Enjoy immediately or store in a reusable container in the refrigerator for up to 5 days.

Per Serving

calories: 944 | fat: 33.1g | carbs: 139.8g | protein: 34.2g | fiber: 38.1g

Simple Chickpea Salad Sandwich

Prep time: 5 minutes | Cook time: 0 minutes | Serves 2

- 2 cups cooked chickpeas
- ½ block firm tofu, chopped
- 1 celery stalk, chopped
- 1 scallion, chopped
- 3 tablespoons vegan mayonnaise
- 1 tablespoon yellow mustard
- ⅛ teaspoon freshly ground black pepper
- Pink Himalayan salt, to taste (optional)
- 4 slices whole wheat bread

1. In a large bowl, mash the chickpeas.
2. Add the tofu, celery, scallion, mayo, mustard, pepper, and salt (if using) and mix well.
3. Spread the salad equally on 2 slices of bread and top with the remaining slices to make 2 sandwiches.
4. Serve immediately.

Per Serving

calories: 618 | fat: 14.8g | carbs: 93.9g | protein: 33.1g | fiber: 19.2g

Black Bean and Avocado Salad

Prep time: 5 minutes | Cook time: 0 minutes | Serves 2

- 2 cups cooked black beans
- 1 avocado, pitted, peeled, and chopped
- ½ cup corn
- 1 small tomato, chopped
- 2 scallions, chopped
- 2 tablespoons diced jalapeños
- ⅛ cup chopped fresh cilantro
- 1 tablespoon freshly squeezed lime juice
- Pink Himalayan salt, to taste (optional)

1. In a large bowl, combine the beans, avocado, corn, tomato, scallions, jalapeños, and cilantro and mix well with a wooden spoon. Sprinkle with the lime juice and a pinch of salt (if using) and enjoy.

Per Serving

calories: 854 | fat: 30.1g | carbs: 123.2g | protein: 38.3g | fiber: 45.9g

5-Bean Chili

Prep time: 15 minutes | Cook time: 1 hour | Serves 8

- 2 (26- to 28-ounce / 737- to 794-g) cans diced tomatoes
- 1 (19-ounce / 539-g) can red kidney beans, drained and rinsed
- 1 (19-ounce / 539-g) can white kidney beans, drained and rinsed
- 1 (19-ounce / 539-g) can chickpeas, drained and rinsed
- 1 (19-ounce / 539-g) can black beans, drained and rinsed
- 1 (19-ounce / 539-g) can pinto beans, drained and rinsed
- 2½ cups fresh mushrooms, sliced
- 1 medium red bell pepper, chopped
- 1 large yellow onion, chopped
- 1 cup corn, canned or frozen
- 1½ tablespoons chili powder
- 1 teaspoon ground cumin
- ½ teaspoon freshly ground black pepper
- ½ teaspoon pink Himalayan salt
- ¼ teaspoon cayenne pepper
- ¼ teaspoon garlic powder

1. Combine all the ingredients in a large pot over medium heat. Cover the pot with a lid and cook, stirring occasionally, for 45 to 60 minutes.
2. Serve as is, or on a bed of brown rice, quinoa, or with a fresh avocado.

Per Serving

calories: 757 | fat: 5.3g | carbs: 139.1g | protein: 41.2g | fiber: 44.2g

Sumptuous Buddha Bowl

Prep time: 15 minutes | Cook time: 20 to 22 minutes | Serves 1

For the Vegetables:

- 1 small sweet potato, cubed
- Freshly ground black pepper, to taste
- Pink Himalayan salt, to taste
- 2 cups stemmed and chopped kale
- ½ cup edamame
- 1 small bunch broccolini
- 1 avocado, pitted, peeled, and sliced
- ½ cup cooked quinoa

For the Ginger-Tahini Sauce:

- 1-inch fresh ginger root, minced
- 1 garlic clove, minced
- 2 tablespoons tahini
- 2 tablespoons water
- 1 tablespoon freshly squeezed lemon juice
- ½ tablespoon red wine vinegar
- ½ teaspoon low-sodium soy sauce

Optional Toppings:

- ½ cup cooked chickpeas
- ½ cup shredded purple cabbage
- 1 tablespoon shelled pumpkin seeds

1. Preheat the oven to 400ºF (205ºC). Line a baking sheet with parchment paper or a silicone liner.
2. Spread out the sweet potato on the prepared baking sheet and sprinkle evenly with the pepper and salt. Cook for 15 minutes, or until lightly browned.
3. Steam the kale, edamame, and broccolini for 5 to 7 minutes, or until softened.
4. In a medium bowl, combine all the ingredients for the ginger-tahini sauce and mix well.
5. In a large bowl, arrange the vegetables and the avocado over the quinoa and drizzle with the sauce. Sprinkle with the toppings (if using).

Per Serving

calories: 947 | fat: 49.1g | carbs: 106.9g | protein: 32.2g | fiber: 30.1g

Air-Fried Seitan

Prep time: 10 minutes | Cook time: 1 hour | Serves 2

- 1 cup vital wheat gluten
- 2 tablespoons whole wheat flour
- 1 teaspoon vegan poultry seasoning
- 1 tablespoon nutritional yeast
- 1 teaspoon onion powder
- 1 teaspoon garlic powder
- ¼ teaspoon pink Himalayan salt
- Pinch of freshly ground black pepper
- 1 tablespoon aquafaba (the liquid from a can of chickpeas)
- 6¾ cups water, divided
- 1 vegan not-chick'n bouillon cube

1. In a large bowl, mix the gluten, flour, poultry seasoning, nutritional yeast, onion powder, garlic powder, salt, and pepper. Stir in the aquafaba and ¾ cup of water.
2. Knead the seitan dough together until the ingredients are mixed well. Transfer to a cutting board, roll out, and cut into 1-by-2-inch strips.
3. In a large pot over high heat, bring the remaining 6 cups of water and the bouillon cube to a boil. Reduce the heat to medium low. Add the seitan strips and simmer for 30 minutes. Drain the broth from the seitan pieces when ready to transfer to the air fryer.
4. Put the seitan strips in the air fryer and cook at 370ºF (188ºC) for 20 to 30 minutes, or until golden brown.
5. Serve immediately or store in a sealed container for up to 7 days.

Per Serving

calories: 274 | fat: 2.3g | carbs: 18.9g | protein: 48.2g | fiber: 3.3g

Zoodles with Crunchy Sesame Tofu

Prep time: 15 minutes | Cook time: 5 minutes | Serves 2

- 3 tablespoons sesame oil, divided
- 2 cups firm tofu, cubed
- ¼ cup soy sauce
- 2 medium zucchinis, sliced into noodles
- 2 tablespoons roasted sesame seeds (optional)
- 1 green onion, sliced (optional)

Sesame Peanut Topping:

- ½ cup peanut butter
- ¼ cup soy sauce
- ¼ cup rice vinegar
- 2 teaspoons chili flakes
- 2 tablespoons maple syrup
- 1 inch fresh ginger, peeled, chopped
- 3 garlic cloves

1. Put a large skillet on medium heat and add 2 tablespoons of sesame oil.
2. Put in the cubed tofu and sauté for 5 minutes until light brown.
3. Add the first ¼ cup of soy sauce and stir well.
4. Turn the heat down to low and allow the tofu to absorb the soy sauce until the tofu is slightly crisp.
5. Put the crispy tofu aside for later use.
6. Take a blender and mix all the sesame peanut topping ingredients.
7. Mix the tofu with the sesame peanut topping.
8. Serve the raw zucchini noodles with the crispy tofu and sauce in a medium bowl.
9. Top the dish with the optional roasted sesame seeds and green onion slices.
10. Serve immediately or store the ingredients separately!

Per Serving

calories: 655 | fat: 41.8g | carbs:35.5g | protein: 33.8g | fiber: 9.2g

Asian Noodles with Nutty Tofu Crisp

Prep time: 10 minutes | Cook time: 10 minutes | Serves 4

- ¼ cup rice or balsamic vinegar
- 1 tablespoon soy sauce
- 2 tablespoons natural peanut butter
- 2 cloves garlic, minced
- 1 bunch green onions, finely chopped
- 1 teaspoon Asian chili paste
- 1 tablespoon water
- 1 teaspoon sugar
- 16 ounces (454 g) extra-firm tofu, cut in half horizontally, pressed to remove extra water
- 12 ounces (340 g) thin spaghetti, cut in half (regular or whole wheat)
- 1 tablespoon finely chopped peanuts
- 1 teaspoon peanut or canola oil

1. Mix the first eight ingredients with a fork to create marinade.
2. Cut pressed tofu halves a second time, diagonally. Place tofu quarters in marinade for at least 15 minutes on each side.
3. Bring a large pot of water to a boil. Stir in the noodles and cook for 6 minutes. Drain the noodles and set aside.
4. Dip the marinated tofu into the chopped peanuts to fully coat one side. Heat 1 teaspoon of peanut oil in a nonstick skillet. Cook tofu for 1 to 2 minutes, with the peanut side down, until golden brown and repeat on the other side.
5. Heat remaining marinade over the stove or in the microwave and pour over the hot noodles. Divide noodles into four equal servings, place nutty tofu cakes on top, and serve.

Per Serving

calories: 339 | fat: 12.6g | carbs:36.1g | protein: 30.2g | fiber: 4.0g

Kale Slaw Tacos

Prep time: 15 minutes | Cook time: 0 minutes | Serves 3

Filling:

- 1 tablespoon taco seasoning
- 3 tablespoons tamari
- 8 ounces (227 g) extra-firm tofu, drained, pressed, and cut into ½-inch chunks
- 1 (15-ounce / 425-g) can pinto beans, drained and rinsed
- ¼ cup finely diced white onion
- 2 Roma tomatoes, finely diced
- ½ teaspoon salt
- Pinch of ground black pepper
- 1 teaspoon chopped parsley

Kale Slaw:

- 1 cup stemmed and coarsely chopped kale
- 1 tablespoon lemon juice
- 1 cup thinly sliced purple cabbage
- 1 cup thinly sliced green cabbage
- ¼ cup shredded carrots
- 2 tablespoons vegan mayonnaise
- 1 tablespoon lime juice
- 1 teaspoon maple syrup
- 1 chipotle pepper in adobo sauce, chopped finely

To Assemble:

- 6 taco shells

1. Mix the taco seasoning and tamari in a small bowl. Set aside.
2. Add the tofu to the tamari mixture and toss. Marinate while working on the bean mixture and slaw.
3. Add the beans, onion, tomatoes, salt, pepper, and parsley to a small bowl. Toss and set aside to meld.
4. Add the kale to a medium bowl and add the lemon juice. Massage the kale with your hands to soften it up. Add both cabbages, the carrots, mayonnaise, lime juice, maple syrup, and chili in adobo sauce. Mix well.
5. Assemble the tacos by layering the shells with the bean mixture, tofu, and finally the slaw.

Per Serving

calories: 404 | fat: 14.3g | carbs: 52.4g | protein: 20.4g | fiber: 11.0g

Tacos with Tempeh and Baked Cauliflower

Prep time: 10 minutes | Cook time: 22 to 32 minutes | Serves 4

- 8 ounces (227 g) original tempeh
- 3 tablespoons hot sauce, divided
- ¼ cup plus 2 tablespoons unsweetened almond milk, divided
- 1 small head cauliflower
- 1 cup whole wheat flour
- 2 tablespoons taco seasoning
- ½ cup panko bread crumbs
- 2 tablespoons nutritional yeast
- 1 tablespoon coconut oil
- 2 cups shredded romaine lettuce
- 8 taco shells
- 2 Roma tomatoes, chopped
- Lime wedges (optional)
- Salsa (optional)

1. Preheat the oven to 350ºF (180ºC).
2. Cut the tempeh widthwise into ¼-inch strips, then tear those into about ½-inch pieces.
3. Mix 1 tablespoon of the hot sauce and 2 tablespoons of the milk together in a small bowl. Add tempeh and toss. Let marinate for 1 hour.
4. Meanwhile, prepare the cauliflower by cutting the florets into small bite-size pieces.
5. Mix 2 tablespoons of hot sauce and ¼ cup milk in a large bowl. Add the cauliflower and toss.
6. Add the flour, taco seasoning, panko, and nutritional yeast to a large bowl and mix well.
7. Take the cauliflower out of the wet mixture and add to the flour mixture and toss to coat all of the florets. Place on a baking sheet and bake for 20 to 30 minutes, turning after 15 minutes. You will be able to pierce them easily with a fork when done.
8. While the cauliflower is baking, heat the oil in a small skillet over medium-high heat and add the tempeh. Cook for about 2 minutes, flipping occasionally, until the pieces become golden brown. Remove from the heat to a paper towel.
9. Assemble the taco by laying some lettuce in the bottom of a shell and spooning in some tempeh, cauliflower, and tomato. Serve with lime wedges and salsa, if desired.

Per Serving

calories: 495 | fat: 17.6g | carbs: 67.1g | protein: 22.9g | fiber: 10.6g

Spicy Soba Noodles with Peanut Sauce

Prep time: 15 minutes | Cook time: 8 minutes | Serves 4

For the Peanut Sauce:

- ¼ cup smooth peanut butter
- ¼ cup warm water
- ¼ cup tamari
- 2 tablespoons pure maple syrup
- 1 tablespoon lime zest
- Juice of 1 lime
- 2 garlic cloves, minced
- 1 tablespoon grated peeled fresh ginger
- 2 tablespoons red pepper sauce, like sriracha

For the Noodle Bowls:

- 1 cup shelled edamame, thawed if frozen
- 1 carrot, shredded
- 1 shallot, thinly sliced
- 1 red bell pepper, cut into strips
- 1 small red cabbage head, chopped
- 1 bunch spring onions, chopped, divided
- ½ cup unsalted peanuts
- 1 (9.5-ounce / 269-g) package soba noodles
- 1 tablespoon toasted sesame seeds
- Chopped fresh cilantro, for serving

1. Make the peanut sauce: In a small bowl, whisk together the peanut butter, warm water, tamari, maple syrup, lime zest and juice, garlic, ginger, and pepper sauce until smooth. The sauce can also be puréed in a blender for even easier preparation. Set aside.
2. In a large bowl, toss together the edamame, carrot, shallot, bell pepper, red cabbage, three-quarters of the spring onions, and peanuts.
3. Bring a large pot of water to a boil. Stir in the soba noodles and cook for 8 minutes. Drain and rinse the noodles.
4. Add the noodles to the mixed vegetables and pour on three-quarters of the peanut sauce. Using tongs or pasta spoons, mix to combine. Serve with a drizzle of the remaining sauce on top, a sprinkle of toasted sesame seeds, a pinch of cilantro, and the remaining spring onions.

Per Serving

calories: 625 | fat: 21.8g | carbs: 84.1g | protein: 31.2g | fiber: 8.9g

Brown Rice and Black Bean Burritos

Prep time: 10 minutes | Cook time: 5 minutes | Serves 4

For the Seasoning:

- 1 tablespoon chili powder
- 1 teaspoon paprika
- 1 teaspoon ground cumin
- ½ teaspoon garlic powder
- ½ teaspoon onion powder
- ¼ teaspoon freshly ground black pepper
- ¼ teaspoon red pepper flakes
- ⅛ teaspoon dried oregano
- ⅛ teaspoon salt

For the Burritos:

- 1 cup low-sodium vegetable broth
- ¼ cup water
- 1 cup dried TVP (textured vegetable protein)
- 4 large gluten-free tortillas
- 2 cups cooked brown rice
- 2 cups cooked black beans
- 2 cups shredded lettuce
- 1 cup fresh corn
- Pico de Gallo, for topping (optional)
- Avocado or guacamole, for topping (optional)
- Salsa, for topping (optional)

1. In a small bowl, combine all the ingredients for the seasoning and stir well. Set aside.
2. In a nonstick pan over high heat, bring the broth and water to a boil. Add the TVP and the seasoning and combine. Reduce the heat to low, cover the pan, and simmer, stirring frequently, for 5 minutes, or until the TVP has absorbed all the moisture and is soft.
3. On a large plate, place 1 tortilla and top with one-quarter of the TVP mixture, rice, beans, lettuce, corn, and toppings (if using). Fold in the sides of the tortilla and roll it up. Repeat with the remaining tortillas and ingredients.
4. Serve immediately.

Per Serving

calories: 655 | fat: 8.2g | carbs: 110.9g | protein: 34.2g | fiber: 24.1g

Spiced Veggie Fajitas

Prep time: 10 minutes | Cook time: 10 minutes | Serves 4

- 1 tablespoon chili powder
- ½ tablespoon garlic powder
- 1 teaspoon onion powder
- ½ teaspoon ground cumin
- ½ teaspoon paprika
- ½ teaspoon cayenne pepper
- 1 red onion, sliced
- ½ red bell pepper, sliced
- ½ green bell pepper, sliced
- 1 garlic clove, minced
- ¼ cup low-sodium vegetable broth
- 2 cups cooked black beans
- 1 cup sliced mushrooms
- 8 (8-inch) whole wheat tortillas

1. In a small bowl, mix the chili powder, garlic powder, onion powder, cumin, paprika, and cayenne pepper.
2. In a medium nonstick pan over medium-high heat, sauté the onion, red and green bell peppers, and garlic in the broth for 5 minutes, covered, stirring occasionally. Add the seasoning mix, black beans, and mushrooms. Stir and cook for another 5 minutes.
3. Divide the veggies equally among the tortillas and enjoy immediately or store the veggies in the refrigerator for up to 5 days.

Per Serving

calories: 826 | fat: 14.1g | carbs: 144.9g | protein: 35.3g | fiber: 32.1g

Pasta with Ricotta Red Sauce

Prep time: 5 minutes | Cook time: 13 minutes | Serves 4

- 1 block firm tofu
- 1 cup cashews, soaked for 1 hour in hot water
- 1 cup fresh spinach
- 1 cup chopped mushrooms
- 4 garlic cloves
- 1½ tablespoons nutritional yeast
- 1 tablespoon freshly squeezed lemon juice
- 1 teaspoon dried oregano
- ½ teaspoon dried basil
- ¼ teaspoon pink Himalayan salt
- ⅛ teaspoon freshly ground black pepper
- 10 ounces (284 g) chickpea-based pasta
- 1½ cups vegan red pasta sauce
- Parmesan Cheese, for topping (optional)

1. In a food processor, blend the tofu, cashews, spinach, mushrooms, garlic, nutritional yeast, lemon juice, oregano, basil, salt, and pepper until smooth.

2. In a large pot of boiling water, cook the pasta for 8 minutes. Drain.
3. In a large nonstick pan over medium-low heat, combine the cashew ricotta with the pasta sauce and cook for 5 minutes. Add the pasta and stir. Sprinkle with Parmesan cheese (if using). Serve immediately.

Per Serving

calories: 609 | fat: 28.2g | carbs:65.9g | protein: 36.3g | fiber: 16.2g

Crispy Baked Tempeh

Prep time: 5 minutes | Cook time: 25 minutes | Serves 2

- 1 (14-ounce / 397-g) pack tempeh, cubed
- ¼ cup low-sodium soy sauce
- ¼ cup lemon juice
- 4-inch piece ginger, minced
- 4 cloves garlic, minced

Optional Toppings:

- Sauerkraut
- Shredded coconut

1. Put the tempeh cubes in an airtight container with all the other ingredients, except for the optional toppings.
2. Close the lid and shake well until the tempeh cubes are evenly covered with the marinade.
3. Put the airtight container in the refrigerator for at least 2 hours, and up to 24 hours, to make sure the tempeh is thoroughly marinated.
4. Preheat the oven to 375°F (190°C) and line a baking sheet with parchment paper.
5. Transfer the tempeh cubes onto the baking sheet and bake for about 25 minutes or until the tempeh is browned and crispy.
6. Serve the tempeh with the optional toppings and enjoy!

Per Serving

calories: 430 | fat: 19.3g | carbs:10.4g | protein: 47.8g | fiber: 11.7g

Chapter 6

Snacks and Sides

76	Veggie-Loaded Baked Sweet Potatoes
76	Lentil and Kale Stew
77	Cookie Dough Oats
77	Spiced Split Pea Soup
78	Mocha Chocolate Brownie Bars
78	Crispy Kale Chips
79	Avocado-Strawberry Toast
79	Crispy Cauliflower Florets
80	Pistachio Energy Bites
80	Peanut Oatmeal Cookies
81	Walnut Cranberry Power Cookies
81	Peppermint-Chocolate Nice Cream
82	Chocolate Sunflower Seed Balls
82	Coconut Lemon Protein Bites
83	Plantain Mango Nice Cream
83	Fresh Mango Salsa
84	Simple Chickpea Guacamole
84	Fast and Easy Corn Salsa
85	Carrot, Barley and Spinach Soup
86	Leek and Asparagus Soup

Snacks and Sides | 75

Veggie-Loaded Baked Sweet Potatoes

Prep time: 5 minutes | Cook time: 1 hour | Serves 2

- 2 sweet potatoes
- 2 cups fresh kale
- 1 cup cooked black beans (drained and rinsed, if canned)
- ½ cup corn, frozen or canned
- ½ small red onion, diced
- ¼ cup low-sodium vegetable broth or water
- ¾ cup chopped fresh tomatoes
- 1 teaspoon chopped fresh cilantro

1. Preheat the oven to 400°F (205°C).
2. Poke several holes all over the sweet potatoes with a fork. Bake on a baking sheet for 50 minutes, or until tender.
3. While the potatoes are cooking, warm the kale, beans, corn, and onion in a nonstick pan over medium heat with the broth, covered with a lid but stirring frequently, for 10 minutes, or until the onion has softened.
4. Remove the potatoes from the oven, cut down the center of each, and push the ends toward each other to open up the potato. Place the vegetable mixture on top. Add the tomatoes and cilantro, and serve immediately.

Per Serving

calories: 684 | fat: 4.2g | carbs: 142.8g | protein: 29.1g | fiber: 32.2g

Lentil and Kale Stew

Prep time: 10 minutes | Cook time: 45 minutes | Serves 8

- 5 cups brown or green dry lentils
- 8 cups low-sodium vegetable broth or water
- 4 cups kale, stemmed and chopped into 2-inch pieces
- 2 large carrots, diced
- 1 tablespoon smoked paprika
- 2 teaspoons onion powder
- 2 teaspoons garlic powder
- 1 teaspoon red pepper flakes
- 1 teaspoon dried oregano
- 1 teaspoon dried thyme

1. In a large stockpot, combine the lentils, broth, kale, carrots, paprika, onion powder, garlic powder, red pepper flakes, oregano, and thyme. Bring to a boil over medium-high heat.
2. Cover, reduce the heat to medium-low, and simmer for 45 minutes, stirring every 5 to 10 minutes. Serve warm.

Per Serving

calories: 468 | fat: 3.2g | carbs: 77.9g | protein: 32.3g | fiber: 30.8g

Cookie Dough Oats

Prep time: 5 minutes | Cook time: 0 minutes | Serves 2

- ½ cup quick or rolled oats
- 1 tablespoon flaxseeds
- 2 scoops vanilla flavor vegan protein powder
- 1 cup unsweetened almond milk
- 1 tablespoon peanut butter
- 1 tablespoon carob chips (optional)
- 1 tablespoon maple syrup (optional)

1. Take a lidded bowl or jar and add the oats, flaxseed, protein powder, and almond milk.
2. Stir until everything is thoroughly combined and the mixture looks runny; if not, add a little more almond milk.
3. Blend in the peanut butter with a spoon until everything is mixed well.
4. Place or close the lid on the bowl or jar and transfer it to the refrigerator.
5. Allow the jar to sit overnight or for at least five hours, so the flavors can set.
6. Serve the dough oats, and if desired, topped with the optional carob chips and a small cap of maple syrup.
7. Serve immediately.

Per Serving

calories: 317 | fat: 11.4g | carbs: 22.8g | protein: 30.8g | fiber: 4.3g

Spiced Split Pea Soup

Prep time: 5 minutes | Cook time: 45 minutes | Serves 6

- 1 (16-ounce / 454-g) package dried green split peas, soaked overnight
- 5 cups low-sodium vegetable broth or water
- 2 teaspoons garlic powder
- 2 teaspoons onion powder
- 1 teaspoon dried oregano
- 1 teaspoon dried thyme
- ¼ teaspoon freshly ground black pepper

1. In a large stockpot, combine the split peas, broth, garlic powder, onion powder, oregano, thyme, and pepper. Bring to a boil over medium-high heat.
2. Cover, reduce the heat to medium-low, and simmer for 45 minutes, stirring every 5 to 10 minutes. Serve warm.

Per Serving

calories: 298 | fat: 2.1g | carbs: 48.2g | protein: 23.3g | fiber: 19.8g

Mocha Chocolate Brownie Bars

Prep time: 5 minutes | Cook time: 0 minutes | Serves 3

- 2½ cups vegan protein powder (chocolate or vanilla)
- ½ cup cocoa powder
- ½ cup old-fashioned or quick oats
- ¼ teaspoon nutmeg
- 2 tablespoons agave nectar
- 1 teaspoon pure vanilla extract
- 1 cup brewed coffee (cold)

1. Line a square baking dish with parchment paper and set it aside.
2. Mix the dry ingredients together in a large bowl.
3. Slowly incorporate the agave nectar, vanilla extract, and cold coffee while stirring constantly until all the lumps in the mixture have disappeared.
4. Pour the batter into the dish, while making sure to press it into the corners.
5. Place the dish into the refrigerator until firm, or for about 4 hours. Alternatively use the freezer for just 1 hour.
6. Slice the chunk into 6 even squares, and serve.

Per Serving

calories: 214 | fat: 3.9g | carbs: 17.4g | protein: 27.3g | fiber: 3.8g

Crispy Kale Chips

Prep time: 5 minutes | Cook time: 20 minutes | Serves 4

- ¼ cup low-sodium vegetable broth
- 1 tablespoon nutritional yeast
- ½ teaspoon garlic powder
- ½ teaspoon onion powder
- 6 ounces (170 g) kale, stemmed and cut into 2- to 3-inch pieces

1. Preheat the oven to 300°F (150°C). Line a baking sheet with parchment paper.
2. In a small bowl, mix together the broth, nutritional yeast, garlic powder, and onion powder.
3. Put the kale in a large bowl. Pour the broth and seasonings over the kale, and toss well to thoroughly coat.
4. Place the kale pieces on the baking sheet in an even layer. Bake for 20 minutes, or until crispy, turning the kale halfway through.
5. Serve warm.

Per Serving

calories: 42 | fat: 0g | carbs: 7.2g | protein: 4.4g | fiber: 2.1g

Avocado-Strawberry Toast

Prep time: 5 minutes | Cook time: 0 minutes | Serves 4

- 1 avocado, peeled, pitted, and quartered
- 4 whole-wheat bread slices, toasted
- 4 ripe strawberries, cut into ¼-inch slices
- 1 tablespoon balsamic glaze or reduction

1. Mash one-quarter of the avocado on a slice of toast. Layer one-quarter of the strawberry slices over the avocado, and finish with a drizzle of balsamic glaze. Repeat with the remaining ingredients, and serve.

Per Serving

calories: 151 | fat: 8.2g | carbs: 17.1g | protein: 5.3g | fiber: 5.2g

Crispy Cauliflower Florets

Prep time: 5 minutes | Cook time: 40 minutes | Serves 6

- 1 cup oat milk
- ¾ cup gluten-free or whole-wheat flour
- 2 teaspoons garlic powder
- 2 teaspoons onion powder
- ½ teaspoon paprika
- ¼ teaspoon freshly ground black pepper
- 1 head cauliflower, cut into bite-size florets

1. Preheat the oven to 425ºF (220ºC). Line a baking sheet with parchment paper.
2. In a large bowl, whisk together the milk, flour, garlic powder, onion powder, paprika, and pepper. Add the cauliflower florets, and mix until the florets are completely coated.
3. Place the coated florets on the baking sheet in an even layer, and bake for 40 minutes, or until golden brown and crispy, turning once halfway through the cooking process. Serve.

Per Serving

calories: 97 | fat: 1.1g | carbs: 20.2g | protein: 3.4g | fiber: 2.1g

Pistachio Energy Bites

Prep time: 5 minutes | Cook time: 0 minutes | Makes 18 balls

- ½ cup old-fashioned oats
- ½ cup almond butter
- ¼ cup maple syrup
- ⅓ cup oat bran
- ⅓ cup flaxseed meal
- ⅓ cup pistachios, ground
- 1 tablespoon raw shelled hempseed

1. Add all the ingredients to a large bowl and mix well.
2. Roll into eighteen balls. Serve.

Per Serving (2 balls)

calories: 195 | fat: 12.2g | carbs: 18.6g | protein: 6.5g | fiber: 4.6g

Peanut Oatmeal Cookies

Prep time: 5 minutes | Cook time: 11 minutes | Serves 12

- 1 tablespoon chia seeds or ground chia seeds
- 3 tablespoons water
- 1 cup whole wheat flour
- 1 teaspoon baking powder
- 1½ cups old-fashioned oats
- 2 tablespoons vanilla protein powder
- ½ cup peanut butter
- 1 cup coconut sugar
- ½ cup dairy-free cream cheese, softened
- 1 teaspoon vanilla extract
- 1 banana
- 1 cup peanuts, chopped

1. Preheat the oven to 400°F (205°C). Cut parchment paper to fit on a baking sheet. Set aside.
2. Mix the chia seeds with the water and set aside.
3. Add the flour, baking powder, oats, and protein powder to a large bowl. Set aside.
4. Add the butter and sugar to the bowl of a stand mixer. Cream on medium-low speed for 5 minutes. Add the cream cheese and mix well. Turn off the beater and add the prepared chia seed mixture, vanilla, and banana. Mix well on medium speed. Add the dry ingredients and peanuts and keep mixing until just combined.
5. Spoon dollops on a cookie sheet, 2 inches apart, and flatten with the bottom of a glass to about ½-inch thick. Bake for 11 minutes.
6. Cool on a wire rack. Serve immediately.

Per Serving

calories: 274 | fat: 10.1g | carbs: 36.9g | protein: 11.4g | fiber: 4.9g

Walnut Cranberry Power Cookies

Prep time: 5 minutes | Cook time: 10 minutes | Serves 12

- 1 cup peanut butter, softened
- 1 cup coconut sugar
- ⅓ cup orange juice
- 2 teaspoons organic vanilla extract
- 1½ cups whole wheat flour
- 2 tablespoons protein powder
- 1 teaspoon baking powder
- ¼ teaspoon baking soda
- 1 cup old-fashioned oats
- 1 cup dairy-free chocolate chips
- 1 cup chopped walnuts
- 1 cup dried cranberries

1. Preheat the oven to 375ºF (190ºC).
2. Beat the butter and sugar together in the bowl of a stand mixer. Add the orange juice and vanilla extract. Mix well.
3. Add flour, protein powder, baking powder, and baking soda to a medium bowl. Mix and add to the wet mixture. Mix on medium speed until well blended. Add the oats, chocolate chips, walnuts, and cranberries. Mix on low.
4. Drop heaping tablespoons, about 2 inches apart, on an ungreased baking sheet. These are big cookies. They spread out to 3 to 4 inches in diameter. Bake for 10 to 11 minutes.
5. Cool for a minute and then transfer to a wire rack to cool completely.
6. Serve immediately.

Per Serving (2 cookies)

calories: 302 | fat: 10.0g | carbs: 47.8g | protein: 8.1g | fiber: 4.6g

Peppermint-Chocolate Nice Cream

Prep time: 5 minutes | Cook time: 0 minutes | Serves 2

- 3 frozen ripe bananas, broken into thirds
- 3 tablespoons plant-based milk
- 2 tablespoons cocoa powder
- ⅛ teaspoon peppermint extract

1. In a food processor, combine the bananas, milk, cocoa powder, and peppermint.
2. Process on medium speed for 30 to 60 seconds, or until the bananas have been blended into smooth soft-serve consistency, and serve.

Per Serving

calories: 174 | fat: 2.2g | carbs: 42.8g | protein: 3.3g | fiber: 6.2g

Chocolate Sunflower Seed Balls

Prep time: 5 minutes | Cook time: 0 minutes | Serves 16

- 16 ounces (454 g) dairy-free chocolate chips
- ½ cup creamy peanut butter
- ½ cup raw shelled hempseed
- ½ cup unsweetened shredded coconut
- 1 cup sunflower seed kernels, pulsed fine in a mini food processor, divided

1. Melt the chocolate in a double boiler. Stir in the peanut butter and blend well. Take off the heat and mix in the hempseed, shredded coconut, and ½ cup sunflower seeds. Refrigerate until the dough is firm enough to use a small cookie scoop, about 30 minutes.
2. Remove the dough from the refrigerator and scoop out forty-eight balls. You can roll them into smoother balls with the palms of your hands. While they are still warm from rolling, roll them in the remaining pulsed sunflower seeds.
3. Serve.

Per Serving

calories: 178 | fat: 11.9g | carbs: 14.7g | protein: 5.8g | fiber: 1.8g

Coconut Lemon Protein Bites

Prep time: 5 minutes | Cook time: 0 minutes | Makes 24 balls

- 1¾ cups cashews
- ¼ cup coconut flour
- ¼ cup unsweetened shredded coconut
- 3 tablespoons raw shelled hempseed
- 3 tablespoons maple syrup
- 3 tablespoons fresh lemon juice

1. Place the cashews in a food processor and process until very fine. Add the rest of the ingredients and process until well blended. Dump the mixture into a large bowl.
2. Take a clump of the dough and squeeze it into a ball. Keep squeezing and working it a few times until a ball is formed and solid.
3. Serve.

Per Serving (2 balls)

calories: 158 | fat: 11.4g | carbs: 11.3g | protein: 5.0g | fiber: 1.2g

Plantain Mango Nice Cream

Prep time: 5 minutes | Cook time: 0 minutes | Serves 4

- 2 plantains, peeled, cut into slices, and frozen
- 1 cup frozen mango pieces
- ½ cup unsweetened coconut milk, plus more as needed
- 2 pitted dates or 1 tablespoon pure maple syrup
- 1 teaspoon vanilla extract
- Juice of 1 lime

1. In a high-speed blender or food processor, combine the frozen plantains, mango, milk, dates, vanilla, and lime juice. Blend for 30 seconds. Scrape down the sides and blend again until smooth, scraping down the sides again if the mixture doesn't look smooth. Add more milk, 1 tablespoon at a time, as needed.
2. Refrigerate leftovers in an airtight container for a smoothie-like consistency, or freeze for a firm ice cream texture. If frozen, thaw slightly before serving.

Per Serving (1 cup)

calories: 209 | fat: 1.2g | carbs: 52.2g | protein: 2.3g | fiber: 3.1g

Fresh Mango Salsa

Prep time: 10 minutes | Cook time: 0 minutes | Serves 4

- 2 ripe mangos, peeled, deseeded, and chopped
- ½ red onion, diced
- ½ red bell pepper, diced
- 1 jalapeño pepper, minced
- Juice of 1 lime
- 1 tablespoon packed chopped fresh cilantro

1. In a large bowl, combine the mangos, red onion, bell pepper, jalapeño pepper, lime juice, and cilantro. Stir to combine, while lightly pressing on the mango pieces to break them up.
2. Serve immediately, or refrigerate in a covered bowl for at least 1 hour to allow the flavors to come together. Refrigerate leftovers in an airtight container for up to 1 week.

Per Serving

calories: 115 | fat: 1.2g | carbs: 28.8g | protein: 2.3g | fiber: 3.2g

Simple Chickpea Guacamole

Prep time: 15 minutes | Cook time: 0 minutes | Serves 4

- 1 (15-ounce / 425-g) can chickpeas, drained and rinsed
- 2 large ripe avocados, halved and pitted
- 3 garlic cloves, minced
- ½ small red onion, diced
- ½ small red bell pepper, diced
- ¼ cup packed chopped fresh cilantro
- Juice of 1 lime
- ½ teaspoon ground cumin
- 1 jalapeño pepper, deseeded and minced (optional)

1. Place the chickpeas in a large bowl. Using a potato masher, crush the chickpeas.
2. Scoop the avocado flesh into the bowl of chickpeas and mash to your preferred texture.
3. Using a spatula or spoon, stir in the garlic, red onion, bell pepper, cilantro, lime juice, cumin, and jalapeño pepper (if using). Scoop the guacamole into a sealable container and refrigerate for at least 1 hour to let the flavors combine.
4. Refrigerate leftovers in an airtight container. It is best if eaten within 2 to 3 days but will keep for up 1 week.

Per Serving

calories: 267 | fat: 17.3g | carbs: 26.8g | protein: 7.2g | fiber: 12.3g

Fast and Easy Corn Salsa

Prep time: 15 minutes | Cook time: 0 minutes | Serves 4

- 3 cups fresh corn kernels
- 1 cup quartered grape tomatoes
- 1 green bell pepper, deseeded and diced
- ½ red onion, diced
- ½ cup packed chopped fresh cilantro
- 2 garlic cloves, minced
- Juice of 1 or 2 limes
- ¼ teaspoon freshly ground black pepper

1. In a large bowl, stir together the corn, tomatoes, bell pepper, red onion, cilantro, garlic, lime juice, and pepper. Cover and refrigerate for at least 1 hour before serving.
2. Refrigerate leftovers in an airtight container for up to 1 week.

Per Serving

calories: 144 | fat: 2.2g | carbs: 34.1g | protein: 5.3g | fiber: 5.2g

Carrot, Barley and Spinach Soup

Prep time: 10 minutes | Cook time: 13 minutes | Serves 4

- 6 multicolored carrots, cut into 1-inch pieces
- ½ cup barley
- 1 (15-ounce / 425-g) can diced tomatoes
- 2 garlic cloves, minced
- 4 cups no-sodium vegetable broth
- 2 cups water
- 4 cups fresh spinach
- ¼ cup chopped fresh basil leaves, plus more for garnish
- 2 tablespoons chopped fresh chives, plus more for garnish
- 1 (15-ounce / 425-g) can cannellini beans, rinsed and drained
- 1 tablespoon balsamic vinegar
- Freshly ground black pepper, to taste

1. In a large pot over medium heat, combine the carrots, barley, tomatoes with their juices, garlic, vegetable broth, and water. Bring to a simmer. Cover the pot and cook for 10 minutes, or until the barley is chewy and not hard.
2. Place spinach, basil, and chives on top of the water but do not stir. Cover the pot, reduce heat to low, and cook for 3 minutes to soften the leaves.
3. Stir the pot and add the cannellini beans and vinegar. Remove the pot from the heat and let sit, covered, for 5 minutes. Garnish with chives, basil, and a pinch of pepper to serve.

Per Serving

calories: 262 | fat: 2.2g | carbs: 49.8g | protein: 12.3g | fiber: 14.2g

Leek and Asparagus Soup

Prep time: 10 minutes | Cook time: 27 to 37 minutes | Serves 4

- 2 leeks
- 1 tablespoon water
- 2 garlic cloves, minced
- ¾ teaspoon dried tarragon
- 1 cup dried red lentils
- 1 pound (454 g) asparagus, cut into 1-inch pieces, including the ends
- 6 cups no-sodium vegetable broth
- Juice of 1 lemon
- Fresh ground black pepper, to taste

1. Cut off the leeks' root ends and the dark green portion of the stalks. Slit the remaining white and light green portion lengthwise down the center and run the leeks under cool water, using your fingers to remove any dirt between the layers. Thinly slice the leeks.
2. In a large pot over medium-high heat, combine the leeks and water. Sauté for 5 minutes. Add the garlic and tarragon. Cook for 2 minutes more.
3. Add the lentils, asparagus, and vegetable broth. Bring the soup to a boil, cover the pot, reduce the heat to medium-low, and cook for 20 to 30 minutes until the lentils are tender.
4. Remove some of the cooked lentils, leeks, and asparagus if you'd like some larger pieces in your soup. Using an immersion blender, purée the soup until smooth, or slightly chunky if preferred. Stir in the ingredients removed, if using.
5. Serve with a light drizzle of fresh lemon juice and season with pepper.

Per Serving

calories: 244 | fat: 2.2g | carbs: 44.9g | protein: 16.3g | fiber: 8.2g

Chapter 7

Dinner

89	Garlic-Maple Air-Fried Tofu
89	Veggie Hummus Pizza
90	Sumptuous Minestrone Soup
90	Simple Sushi Bowl
91	Braised Chipotle Tacos
91	Potato Lentil Soup
92	Tofu and Veggie Brown Rice Bowl
92	Vegan Meatballs over Spaghetti
93	Edamame and Asparagus Risotto
94	Hearty Vegetable Pie
95	Tofu Pita with Tzatziki Sauce
96	Teriyaki Veggies and Tofu
96	Mushroom and Tofu Scramble
97	Vegan BLT Sandwich
98	Vegan Meat-Free Loaf
98	Soya Mince and Noodle Bowl
99	Classic Coconut Tofu Curry

88 | Dinner

Garlic-Maple Air-Fried Tofu

Prep time: 5 minutes | Cook time: 20 minutes | Serves 2

- 2 tablespoons low-sodium soy sauce (or tamari, which is a gluten-free option)
- ¼ cup maple syrup
- 6 garlic cloves, minced
- 1 tablespoon apple cider vinegar
- ⅓ teaspoon ground ginger
- ⅛ teaspoon freshly ground black pepper
- 1 block firm tofu, cubed

1. In a medium bowl, combine the soy sauce, maple syrup, garlic, vinegar, ginger, and pepper and stir to mix well. Add the tofu and marinate for at least 10 minutes. The longer the tofu marinates, the more flavor it will absorb.
2. Put the tofu in the air fryer and cook at 375ºF (190ºC) for 18 to 20 minutes, or until the edges are crispy.
3. Enjoy immediately or store in the refrigerator for 5 to 7 days.

Per Serving

calories: 313 | fat: 9.9g | carbs: 38.2g | protein: 23.3g | fiber: 3.1g

Veggie Hummus Pizza

Prep time: 10 minutes | Cook time: 2o to 30 minutes | Makes 2 small pizzas

- ½ zucchini, thinly sliced
- ½ red onion, thinly sliced
- 1 cup cherry tomatoes, halved
- 2 to 4 tablespoons pitted and chopped black olives
- Pinch of sea salt
- Drizzle of olive oil (optional)
- 2 prebaked pizza crusts
- ½ cup hummus
- 2 to 4 tablespoons cashew cheese

1. Preheat the oven to 400ºF (205ºC).
2. Place the zucchini, onion, cherry tomatoes, and olives in a large bowl, sprinkle them with the sea salt, and toss them a bit. Drizzle with a bit of olive oil (if using), to seal in the flavor and keep them from drying out in the oven.
3. Lay the two crusts out on a large baking sheet. Spread half the hummus on each crust, and top with the veggie mixture and cashew cheese.
4. Pop the pizzas in the oven for 20 to 30 minutes, or until the veggies are soft.
5. Serve warm.

Per Serving (1 pizza)

calories: 501 | fat: 25.2g | carbs: 8.3g | protein:19.4 g | fiber: 12.1g

Sumptuous Minestrone Soup

Prep time: 10 minutes | Cook time: 25 to 35 minutes | Serves 6 large bowls

- 1 tablespoon olive oil
- 1 large onion, chopped,
- 5 stalks celery, thinly sliced
- 3 cloves garlic, minced
- 2 bay leaves
- 10 cups water
- 1 to 2 teaspoons iodized salt
- 2 cups fresh tomato purée
- 3 (15-ounce / 425-g) cans beans (combination of kidney, garbanzo, cannellini, butter, or lima beans)
- 3 cups chopped seasonal or frozen vegetables (such as carrots, green beans, potatoes, corn, zucchini, and okra), cut in ½-inch pieces
- ½ cup TVP
- 2 cups fresh or frozen kale, cut in ½-inch strips
- 2 cups cooked small shaped pasta
- 3 tablespoons pesto

1. Sauté onions, garlic, and celery in large soup pot with olive oil.
2. Add water, salt, bay leaves, tomato purée, beans, mixed vegetables, and TVP. Simmer over low for 15 to 20 minutes until all vegetables are tender.
3. Add pasta and kale. Simmer for another 10 to 15 minutes. Stir in the pesto. Note that pasta can also be cooked separately and added at end with the pesto if a firmer texture is desired.
4. Serve warm.

Per Serving

calories: 422 | fat: 9.9g | carbs: 64.8g | protein: 21.2g | fiber: 18.8g

Simple Sushi Bowl

Prep time: 20 minutes | Cook time: 0 minutes | Makes 1 bowl

- ½ cup shelled edamame beans, steamed
- ¾ cup cooked brown rice, or quinoa, millet, or other whole grain
- ½ cup chopped spinach
- ¼ cup sliced avocado
- ¼ cup sliced bell pepper
- ¼ cup chopped fresh cilantro
- 1 scallion, chopped
- ¼ nori sheet
- 1 to 2 tablespoons tamari, or soy sauce
- 1 tablespoon sesame seeds

1. Combine the edamame, rice, spinach, avocado, bell pepper, cilantro, and scallions in a bowl.
2. Cut the nori with scissors into small ribbons and sprinkle on top.
3. Drizzle the bowl with tamari and top with sesame seeds. Serve immediately.

Per Serving

calories: 466 | fat: 20.1g | carbs: 6.3g | protein: 22.1g | fiber: 13.2g

Braised Chipotle Tacos

Prep time: 10 minutes | Cook time: 3 to 4 hours | Serves 4

- 2 (15-ounce / 425-g) cans pinto beans, drained and rinsed
- 1 cup corn, fresh, frozen, or canned
- 3 ounces (85 g) chipotle pepper in adobo sauce (about 2 peppers), chopped
- 6 ounces (170 g) tomato paste
- ¾ cup Thai sweet chili sauce
- 1 tablespoon unsweetened cocoa powder
- 1½ teaspoons taco seasoning
- 8 white corn taco shells or tortillas

Optional Toppings:

- Spinach
- Lettuce
- black olives
- Lime
- Avocado
- Peppers

1. Put everything in the crockpot, except for the taco shells and toppings. Cook on low for 3 to 4 hours or on high for 1½ to 2 hours.
2. Spread the filling on the taco shells. Serve with the toppings, if desired.

Per Serving

calories: 472 | fat: 8.7g | carbs: 81.4g | protein: 20.4g | fiber: 19.0g

Potato Lentil Soup

Prep time: 10 minutes | Cook time: 45 minutes | Serves 4

- 2 medium onions, chopped
- 3 garlic cloves, chopped
- 4 cups water, divided
- 3 small potatoes, chopped
- 1 cup dried brown lentils
- 3 cups chopped kale
- 4 celery stalks, chopped
- 3 medium carrots, chopped
- 1 teaspoon turmeric
- ½ teaspoon freshly ground black pepper
- ½ teaspoon pink Himalayan salt

1. In a large nonstick pot over medium-high heat, sauté the onions and garlic in ¼ cup of water for 5 minutes, or until softened.
2. Add the remaining 3¾ cups of water, the potatoes, lentils, kale, celery, carrots, turmeric, pepper, and salt and stir well. Reduce the heat to medium low, cover, and simmer for 40 minutes, or until the potatoes are soft.
3. Serve warm.

Per Serving

calories: 333 | fat: 1.2g | carbs: 66.2g | protein: 19.3g | fiber: 19.1g

Tofu and Veggie Brown Rice Bowl

Prep time: 10 minutes | Cook time: 30 to 35 minutes | Serves 2

For the Rice:
- 2 cups water
- 1 cup uncooked brown rice
- 1 cup low-sodium vegetable broth
- 1 garlic clove, minced
- 1 teaspoon dried oregano
- ⅛ teaspoon turmeric
- ⅛ teaspoon pink Himalayan salt
- ⅛ teaspoon freshly ground black pepper

For the Tofu and Vegetables:
- 1 block firm tofu, chopped
- ½ cup low-sodium vegetable broth
- ½ cup chopped zucchini
- ½ cup diced red onion
- ½ cup chopped red bell pepper
- 1 medium fresh tomato, chopped
- 1 garlic clove, minced
- ½ teaspoon dried oregano
- ⅛ teaspoon turmeric
- ⅛ teaspoon freshly ground black pepper

1. In a large pot over high heat, combine the water, rice, broth, garlic, oregano, turmeric, salt, and pepper. Bring to a boil. Reduce the heat to low and simmer, covered, for 20 to 25 minutes, or until the rice is soft.
2. In a medium nonstick skillet over medium heat, combine all the ingredients for the tofu and vegetables and cook for 10 minutes, stirring frequently, until soft.
3. Serve the tofu and vegetables on top of the brown rice.

Per Serving

calories: 382 | fat: 9.2g | carbs: 60.9g | protein: 21.3g | fiber: 7.2g

Vegan Meatballs over Spaghetti

Prep time: 10 minutes | Cook time: 25 minutes | Serves 4

- ½ cup TVP (textured vegetable protein)
- ½ cup boiling water
- 2 cups cooked black beans
- 1 cup rolled oats, blended to a flour consistency
- 1 garlic clove, minced
- ½ small yellow onion, diced
- ½ cup cremini mushrooms
- 3 tablespoons aquafaba (the liquid from a can of chickpeas)
- 1 teaspoon Italian seasoning
- ½ teaspoon ground flaxseed
- ½ teaspoon dried oregano
- ½ teaspoon dried basil
- Cooked chickpea-based spaghetti, for serving
- Fresh parsley, for garnish (optional)

1. Preheat the oven to 350ºF (180ºC). Line a baking sheet with parchment paper or a silicone liner.
2. In a small bowl, mix the TVP with the boiling water and let it sit for 5 minutes.
3. In a food processor, combine the TVP, beans, oats, garlic, onion, mushrooms, aquafaba, Italian seasoning, flaxseed, oregano, and basil and pulse until the ingredients are well mixed but not smooth. Don't overblend.
4. Using your hands, form the mixture into 2-inch balls and place them on the prepared baking sheet. Cook in the oven for 20 to 25 minutes, or until lightly browned.
5. Serve with the chickpea-based spaghetti and topped with parsley.

Per Serving (4 meatballs)

calories: 317 | fat: 3.2g | carbs: 51.8g | protein: 22.3g | fiber: 16.2g

Edamame and Asparagus Risotto

Prep time: 15 minutes | Cook time: 40 minutes | Serves 2

- 12 asparagus spears
- 1 small onion, diced
- 3 garlic cloves, minced
- ¾ cup water, divided
- 3 cups low-sodium vegetable broth
- 1 cup uncooked arborio rice
- 1 cup shelled edamame
- 1 red bell pepper, chopped
- 1 tablespoon freshly squeezed lemon juice
- 1 tablespoon apple cider vinegar
- ¾ teaspoon freshly ground black pepper
- ½ teaspoon pink Himalayan salt
- ⅛ teaspoon garlic powder
- ⅛ teaspoon onion powder
- 1 cup unsweetened plant-based milk

1. In a vegetable steamer, cook the asparagus for 5 minutes.
2. In a large nonstick pan over medium-high heat, sauté the onion and garlic in ¼ cup of water for 5 minutes, or until soft. Reduce the heat to medium low, and add the asparagus, broth, rice, edamame, bell pepper, lemon juice, vinegar, pepper, salt, garlic powder, and onion powder and mix well. Cook for 15 minutes.
3. Add the milk and remaining ½ cup of water and stir frequently to blend. The sauce will begin to thicken. Continue to cook for 10 minutes.
4. Reduce the heat to low and simmer, covered, for about 5 minutes, or until the rice is tender.
5. Serve warm.

Per Serving

calories: 549 | fat: 5.3g | carbs: 102.7g | protein: 23.4g | fiber: 9.2g

Hearty Vegetable Pie

Prep time: 15 minutes | Cook time: 50 minutes | Serves 4

- 1 medium yellow onion, diced
- 2 garlic cloves, minced
- 1¼ cups low-sodium vegetable broth, divided
- 3 cups cooked or canned lentils (drained and rinsed, if canned)
- ½ cup frozen peas
- ½ cup frozen carrots
- ½ cup frozen green beans
- ½ cup frozen corn
- 2 tablespoons whole wheat flour
- ⅛ teaspoon plus ½ teaspoon freshly ground black pepper, divided
- 1½ teaspoons dried rosemary
- 1½ teaspoons vegan Worcestershire sauce
- 1 teaspoon tomato paste
- 5 to 6 medium yellow potatoes
- ½ cup unsweetened plant-based milk
- Pink Himalayan salt (optional)
- Smoked paprika (optional)

1. Preheat the oven to 350°F (180°C).
2. In a large nonstick pan over medium-high heat, sauté the onion and garlic in ½ cup of the vegetable broth for 5 minutes, or until soft. Stir in the lentils, peas, carrots, green beans, corn, whole wheat flour, and the remaining ¾ cup of broth. Add ⅛ teaspoon of pepper, the rosemary, Worcestershire sauce, and tomato paste. Cover, reduce the heat to medium low, and cook, stirring occasionally, for 10 minutes.
3. While the vegetables are cooking, in a large pot over high heat, boil the potatoes for 15 minutes, until soft. Drain and mash with the milk and remaining ½ teaspoon of pepper. Add salt to taste (if using).
4. In a 9-by-13-inch casserole dish, evenly spread the vegetable mixture. Spread the mashed potatoes on top. Sprinkle with paprika (if using).
5. Cook in the oven for 20 minutes, or until the mashed potatoes on top are lightly browned.
6. Serve warm.

Per Serving

calories: 383 | fat: 1.2g | carbs: 77.3g | protein: 20.5g | fiber: 17.8g

Tofu Pita with Tzatziki Sauce

Prep time: 15 minutes | Cook time: 15 minutes | Serves 4

- 4 whole wheat pitas

For the Tofu:

- 2 tablespoons freshly squeezed lemon juice
- 1½ tablespoons dried oregano
- 1 tablespoon dried basil
- 1 tablespoon dried dill
- 1 tablespoon onion powder
- 1 tablespoon garlic powder
- ¼ teaspoon dried rosemary
- ⅛ teaspoon pink Himalayan salt
- ¼ teaspoon freshly ground black pepper
- 1 block firm tofu, cubed
- ½ cup low-sodium vegetable broth

For the Tzatziki Sauce:

- 1 cucumber, finely chopped
- 1 cup cashews
- ¼ cup unsweetened plant-based milk
- 3 garlic cloves
- 1½ tablespoons dried dill
- 1 tablespoon freshly squeezed lemon juice
- 2 teaspoons white vinegar

Toppings:

- 1 large tomato, diced
- 2 cups chopped romaine lettuce
- 1 small red onion, thinly sliced

1. In a medium bowl, combine the lemon juice, oregano, basil, dill, onion powder, garlic powder, rosemary, salt, and pepper.
2. In a medium nonstick pan over medium heat, cook the tofu, broth, and spiced lemon juice mixture, covered, for 10 to 15 minutes, stirring frequently.
3. In a food processor, combine all the ingredients for the tzatziki sauce and blend until smooth.
4. Serve the tofu in the pitas, topped with the tomato, lettuce, onion, and tzatziki sauce.

Per Serving

calories: 532 | fat: 23.2g | carbs: 64.8g | protein: 25.2g | fiber: 11.2g

Teriyaki Veggies and Tofu

Prep time: 10 minutes | Cook time: 15 minutes | Serves 2

- ½ cup low-sodium soy sauce (or tamari, which is a gluten-free option)
- ¾ cup plus 1 tablespoon water, divided
- 1-inch fresh ginger root, minced
- 1 garlic clove, minced
- 1 tablespoon apple cider vinegar
- 1 tablespoon coconut sugar
- ½ tablespoon garlic powder
- 1 tablespoon cornstarch
- ½ block firm tofu, cubed
- 2 cups chopped broccoli
- ½ cup grated carrots
- 1 green bell pepper, chopped
- 1 cup snap peas
- 2 cups cooked brown rice
- 2 scallions, chopped, for garnish
- Toasted sesame seeds, for garnish

1. In a small saucepan over medium-low heat, combine the soy sauce, ½ cup of water, ginger, garlic, vinegar, coconut sugar, and garlic powder. Cook for 5 minutes, stirring continuously, until the teriyaki sauce begins to thicken. Set aside.
2. In a small bowl, mix the cornstarch and 1 tablespoon of water into a slurry, and add it to the saucepan. Continue to cook for 2 minutes, stirring to thicken the mixture.
3. In a medium nonstick pan over medium-low heat, sauté the tofu, broccoli, carrots, bell pepper, and snap peas in the remaining ¼ cup of water. Cover and cook for 8 minutes, stirring frequently, or until the vegetables are soft.
4. Add the prepared teriyaki sauce, stirring to mix it thoroughly with the vegetables and tofu.
5. Serve the vegetables and tofu over the rice, garnished with the scallions and sesame seeds.

Per Serving

calories: 480 | fat: 7.2g | carbs: 80.8g | protein: 24.9g | fiber: 11.2g

Mushroom and Tofu Scramble

Prep time: 5 minutes | Cook time: 15 minutes | Serves 4

- 2 cups button mushrooms
- 1 (14-ounce / 397-g) pack extra-firm tofu, scrambled
- ¼ cup low-sodium soy sauce
- ½ cup water
- 2 medium yellow onions, thinly sliced
- ½ cup tahini

Optional Toppings:

- Black pepper
- Parsley
- Lemon slices

1. Add the mushrooms, tofu scramble and soy sauce to an airtight container.
2. Close the lid and shake well until everything is evenly covered with soy sauce.
3. Put the container in the fridge and leave to marinate for at least an hour, or up to 12 hours.
4. Put a large nonstick frying pan over medium heat and add the water and tofu mushroom mixture to the pan.
5. Add the onion slices and cook for about 15 minutes, stirring occasionally with a spatula to prevent the tofu from sticking to the pan, until the mushrooms are cooked and most of the water has evaporated.
6. Turn off the heat and divide the tofu mushroom scramble between 2 bowls.
7. Top the bowls with the tahini, serve with the optional toppings and enjoy!

Per Serving

calories: 340 | fat: 23.4g | carbs:12.7g | protein: 20.2g | fiber: 3.9g

Vegan BLT Sandwich

Prep time: 5 minutes | Cook time: 15 minutes | Serves 2

- 1 (7-ounce / 198-g) pack tempeh, thinly sliced
- ½ cup BBQ sauce
- 2 large tomatoes, sliced
- 4 lettuce leaves
- 4 whole wheat buns

Optional Toppings:

- Guacamole
- BBQ sauce
- Red onion

1. Add the tempeh slices and the BBQ sauce to an airtight container.
2. Close the airtight container, shake well and put it in the fridge, allowing the tempeh to marinate for 1 hour, up to 12 hours.
3. Preheat the oven to 375ºF (190ºC) and line a baking sheet with parchment paper.
4. Transfer the tempeh slices onto the baking sheet and bake for about 15 minutes or until the tempeh is browned and crispy.
5. Bake the buns with the tempeh for the last 5 minutes if you want crispy and browned bread.
6. Spread the guacamole on the bottom half of each bun and add a lettuce leaf on top.
7. Put a quarter of the BBQ tempeh slices on top of the lettuce on each bun and top with 2 slices of tomato on each bun.
8. Cover with the top halves of the buns and serve immediately.

Per Serving

calories: 259 | fat: 9.8g | carbs: 14.7g | protein: 24.2g | fiber: 9.1g

Vegan Meat-Free Loaf

Prep time: 10 minutes | Cook time: 50 minutes | Serves 6

- ¾ cup rolled oats
- 4 cups cooked lentils, divided
- 2 cups chopped mushrooms
- 2 celery stalks, finely chopped
- 1 medium onion, diced
- 2 garlic cloves, minced
- ¼ cup plus 2 tablespoons water, divided
- ½ cup chickpea flour
- 2 tablespoons dried basil
- 1 teaspoon onion powder
- 1 teaspoon garlic powder
- ¼ teaspoon pink Himalayan salt
- ¼ cup organic ketchup
- ½ tablespoon balsamic vinegar
- ½ tablespoon brown sugar

1. Preheat the oven to 350ºF (180ºC). Line a loaf pan with parchment paper or a silicone liner.
2. Put the oats in a food processor and pulse a few times to roughly break them down. Transfer to a large bowl.
3. Put 2 cups of lentils in the food processor and pulse a few times. Transfer to the bowl with the oats.
4. In a medium nonstick pan over medium-high heat, sauté the mushrooms, celery, onion, and garlic in ¼ cup of water for 5 minutes, until the onion is tender. Transfer to the bowl.
5. Add the flour, remaining 2 cups of lentils, basil, onion powder, garlic powder, and salt to the bowl and mix well to combine all the ingredients.
6. Transfer the mixture to the prepared pan and form it into a loaf shape.
7. In a small bowl, combine the remaining 2 tablespoons of water, the ketchup, vinegar, and brown sugar. Spread the sauce on top of the loaf.
8. Cook in the oven for 45 minutes, or until the edges of the loaf are slightly crispy. Serve immediately or store in the refrigerator for up to 5 days.

Per Serving

calories: 387 | fat: 3.2g | carbs: 69.8g | protein: 24.2g | fiber: 21.1g

Soya Mince and Noodle Bowl

Prep time: 10 minutes | Cook time: 13 minutes | Serves 2

- 2 packs brown rice noodles
- 1½ cups water, divided
- ¼ cup low-sodium soy sauce
- 2 yellow onions, minced
- 4 cloves garlic, minced
- 1 (7-ounce / 198-g) pack textured soya mince

Optional Toppings:

- Sauerkraut
- Chili flakes
- Roasted sesame seeds

1. In a large pot of boiling water, cook the noodles for 8 minutes. Drain the excess water with a strainer and set aside.
2. Put a medium pot over medium heat and add ½ cup of the water, soy sauce, minced onion and garlic.
3. Add the soya mince and cook for about 5 minutes, stirring occasionally to prevent the soya mince from sticking to the pan, until the mince has cooked, and half of the water has evaporated.
4. Add the remaining 1 cup of the water and bring to a boil while stirring occasionally.
5. Turn off the heat, add the noodles and stir well until everything is evenly mixed.
6. Divide the noodles and mince between 2 bowls, serve with the optional toppings and enjoy.

Per Serving

calories: 227 | fat: 0.8g | carbs: 26.4g | protein: 25.4g | fiber: 9.5g

Classic Coconut Tofu Curry

Prep time: 10 minutes | Cook time: 20 to 25 minutes | Serves 2

- 1 block firm tofu (14 ounces / 397 g)
- 2 teaspoons coconut oil
- 1 medium sweet onion, diced
- 1½-inch ginger, finely minced
- 1 (13-ounce / 369-g) can reduced-fat unsweetened coconut milk
- 1 cup diced fresh tomatoes
- 1 teaspoon agave nectar (or sweet substitute)
- 1 cup snap peas
- 1 teaspoon curry powder
- 1 teaspoon tumeric
- 1 teaspoon cumin
- ½ teaspoon red pepper flakes
- Salt and pepper, to taste

1. Cut the tofu into ½-inch cubes.
2. Heat the coconut oil in a large skillet over medium-high heat.
3. Add the tofu and cook for about 5 minutes.
4. Stir in the diced onions, and sauté for about 5 to 10 minutes, until the onions are transparent. Add the ginger while stirring.
5. Add in the unsweetened coconut milk, tomatoes, agave nectar, snap peas, and remaining spices.
6. Combine thoroughly, cover, and cook over low heat. Remove after 10 minutes of cooking.
7. Serve immediately, or store the curry in an airtight container to enjoy later.

Per Serving

calories: 450 | fat: 23.2g | carbs:38.6g | protein: 21.9g | fiber: 8.7g

Chapter 8

Desserts

102	Spiced Sweet Potato Cake
102	Microwave Chocolate Mug Cake
103	Chocolate Cookies
103	Peanut Butter Protein Balls
104	Cherry-Chocolate Ice Cream
104	Date and Walnut Chocolate Balls
105	Baked Fruit Crisp
105	Oatmeal and Currant Energy Balls
106	Peanut Butter Scotcheroos
106	Homemade Almond Joys
107	Chocolate Quinoa Bars

Desserts | 101

Spiced Sweet Potato Cake

Prep time: 5 minutes | Cook time: 45 minutes | Serves 6

- 1 sweet potato, cooked and peeled
- ½ cup unsweetened applesauce
- ½ cup plant-based milk
- ¼ cup maple syrup
- 1 teaspoon vanilla extract
- 2 cups whole-wheat flour
- ½ teaspoon baking soda
- ½ teaspoon ground cinnamon
- ¼ teaspoon ground ginger

1. Preheat the oven to 350°F (180°C).
2. In a large mixing bowl, use a fork or potato masher to mash the sweet potato.
3. Mix in the applesauce, milk, maple syrup, and vanilla.
4. Stir in the flour, baking soda, cinnamon, and ginger until the dry ingredients have been thoroughly combined with the wet ingredients.
5. Pour the batter into a nonstick baking dish or one lined with parchment paper. Bake for 45 minutes, or until you can stick a knife into the middle of the cake and it comes out clean.
6. Cool for 5 minutes and slice before serving.

Per Serving

calories: 239 | fat: 1.2g | carbs: 51.9g | protein: 5.2g | fiber: 2.3g

Microwave Chocolate Mug Cake

Prep time: 5 minutes | Cook time: 1 minute | Serves 1

- 3 tablespoons whole-wheat flour
- 3 tablespoons unsweetened applesauce
- 1 tablespoon cocoa powder
- 1 tablespoon maple syrup
- 1 tablespoon plant-based milk
- 1 teaspoon vanilla extract
- ¼ teaspoon baking powder

1. In a microwave-safe coffee mug or bowl, combine the flour, applesauce, cocoa powder, maple syrup, milk, vanilla, and baking powder. Stir together until there are no clumps of dry flour left.
2. Microwave on high for 90 seconds, or until the cake has risen to the top of the mug.
3. Remove from the microwave and set aside to cool for 5 minutes before serving.

Per Serving

calories: 186 | fat: 1.2g | carbs: 40.9g | protein: 4.3g | fiber: 3.2g

Chocolate Cookies

Prep time: 10 minutes | Cook time: 22 minutes | Makes 30 cookies

- ⅓ cup organic cane sugar
- ⅓ cup organic brown sugar
- 4 ounces (113 g) cashew-based vegan butter
- 1 teaspoon vanilla extract
- ½ cup coconut cream
- 1 teaspoon baking soda
- 1 teaspoon baking powder
- 2 tablespoons ground flaxseed
- Pinch of salt
- 2¼ cups almond flour
- ½ cup dairy-free dark chocolate chips

1. Preheat the oven to 325°F (163°C). Line a baking sheet with a silicone baking mat or parchment paper.
2. In a medium bowl or the bowl of a stand mixer, combine the cane sugar, brown sugar, and butter. Using a mixer, cream together.
3. Add the vanilla, coconut cream, baking soda, baking powder, flaxseed, and salt. Mix until well combined.
4. With the mixer running, add the almond flour, a little at a time, until fully incorporated. With a spatula, stir in the chocolate chips.
5. Using a cookie scoop, scoop the cookies onto the prepared baking sheet. Bake for 22 minutes. Let them cool on the tray for a few minutes before transferring to a cooling rack. Serve.

Per Serving (1 cookie)

calories: 131 | fat: 9.9g | carbs: 8.1g | protein: 2.3g | fiber: 1.1g

Peanut Butter Protein Balls

Prep time: 5 minutes | Cook time: 0 minutes | Makes 24 balls

- ½ cup creamy peanut butter
- ½ cup maple syrup
- ½ cup powdered soy milk
- ¼ cup flaxseed meal
- ½ cup coconut flour
- Chopped peanuts, for coating

1. Place the peanut butter and maple syrup in a medium bowl. Mix well. Add the powdered soy milk, flaxseed meal, and coconut flour. Mix well and roll into 24 balls. Lightly roll each ball in the chopped peanuts.
2. Serve immediately. Store in the refrigerator for up to 2 weeks.

Per Serving (2 balls)

calories: 161 | fat: 9.5g | carbs: 14.9g | protein: 6.2g | fiber: 2.2g

Cherry-Chocolate Ice Cream

Prep time: 15 minutes | Cook time: 0 minutes | Serves 6

- 4 frozen bananas (about 14 ounces / 397 g total)
- 1 teaspoon pure vanilla extract
- 2 tablespoons maple syrup
- 2 tablespoons coconut cream
- 2 tablespoons unsweetened almond milk
- 1 cup frozen dark sweet cherries
- ½ cup dairy-free dark chocolate chips

1. In a food processor, combine the bananas, vanilla, maple syrup, coconut cream, and almond milk. Blend until it reaches a batter-like consistency, stopping occasionally to scrape down the sides of the bowl.
2. Scoop out about 1 cup of the banana mixture and place in a freezer-safe container. Add the cherries to the food processor with the remaining banana mixture, and blend until the mixture is pink but you can still see some chunks. Add the chocolate chips and blend again until just combined.
3. Transfer the mixture to the container with the plain banana ice cream and gently stir to create white and pink swirls. Cover and freeze until solid, about 1 hour.
4. Serve chilled.

Per Serving

calories: 253 | fat: 9.9g | carbs: 37.8g | protein: 2.7g | fiber: 2.4g

Date and Walnut Chocolate Balls

Prep time: 5 minutes | Cook time: 0 minutes | Makes 24 balls

- ¾ cup ground sunflower seed kernels
- ½ cup dates, pitted, chopped well
- ½ cup chopped walnuts
- ½ cup unsweetened cacao powder
- ½ cup maple syrup
- ½ cup creamy almond butter
- ½ cup old-fashioned oats
- ¼ cup raw shelled hempseed
- 6 ounces (170 g) unsweetened shredded coconut, for coating

1. Place the sunflower seeds, dates, walnuts, cacao powder, maple syrup, almond butter, oats, and hempseed in a large bowl. Mix well.
2. Pinch off pieces of dough and roll into 24 balls. Roll each ball in the shredded coconut. Place in the refrigerator to harden for about 30 minutes.
3. Serve chilled.

Per Serving (2 balls)

calories: 286 | fat: 19.4g | carbs: 26.5g | protein: 7.4g | fiber: 5.8g

Baked Fruit Crisp

Prep time: 5 minutes | Cook time: 40 to 60 minutes | Serves 12

- 1 cup firmly packed brown sugar
- 1 cup whole-wheat flour
- 2 cups rolled oats
- 2 teaspoons ground cinnamon
- ½ cup canola oil
- 4 to 5 cups fresh or frozen fruit
- 1 teaspoon lemon juice
- 1 teaspoon grated lemon peel

1. Preheat the oven to 350°F (180°C). Lightly grease a 9-inch square baking pan, and set aside.
2. In a small bowl, stir together sugar, flour, oatmeal, and cinnamon. With a pastry blender or fork, cut in oil until mixture is crumbly.
3. Chop fruit and place in baking dish. Sprinkle with lemon peel and lemon juice.
4. Sprinkle crumb mixture evenly over the top.
5. Bake, uncovered, for 40 to 60 minutes until fruit is soft and bubbly. Let cool about 15 minutes before serving.

Per Serving

calories: 276 | fat: 11.2g | carbs: 44.8g | protein: 3.6g | fiber: 4.2g

Oatmeal and Currant Energy Balls

Prep time: 5 minutes | Cook time: 0 minutes | Makes 32 balls

- 1 cup old-fashioned oats
- ¾ cup almond meal
- ⅓ cup wheat germ
- ¼ cup flaxseed meal
- ¼ cup pepitas
- 2 tablespoons raw shelled hempseed
- 1 teaspoon ground cinnamon
- ¼ teaspoon ground nutmeg
- ½ cup dried currants
- ½ cup peanut butter
- ⅓ cup maple syrup
- 1 teaspoon vanilla extract
- ¼ teaspoon salt

1. Mix the oats, almond meal, wheat germ, flaxseed meal, pepitas, hempseed, cinnamon, nutmeg, and currants together in a medium bowl.
2. Add the peanut butter, maple syrup, vanilla, and salt to the bowl of a stand mixer. Mix on medium speed until well combined. Pour the dry ingredients into the wet mixture. Mix on low until well combined.
3. Roll into 32 balls and serve.

Per Serving (2 balls)

calories: 168 | fat: 8.4g | carbs: 19.5g | protein: 5.6g | fiber: 3.5g

Peanut Butter Scotcheroos

Prep time: 5 minutes | Cook time: 4 minutes | Makes 6 scotcheroos

- 1 tablespoon coconut oil
- 2 tablespoons smooth peanut butter
- 2 tablespoons almond flour
- 1 cup gluten-free crispy brown rice cereal
- ½ cup dairy-free dark chocolate chips

1. Line a standard size 6-cup muffin pan with paper baking cups. Set aside.
2. In a small saucepan, melt the coconut oil and peanut butter over medium heat for 1 minute. Add the almond flour and stir until fully incorporated, about 2 minutes. Turn off the heat and add the rice cereal, stirring until fully coated.
3. Divide the rice mixture evenly among the 6 baking cups. Using the bottom of a drinking glass, press the rice mixture firmly into each baking cup to create a dense, even layer.
4. In a small saucepan or double boiler, melt the chocolate over medium-low heat. Stir continuously until fully melted, about 1 minute. Pour the chocolate evenly over the rice mixture, adding an equal amount to each of the 6 cups. Shake and tilt the pan gently from side to side to make sure the chocolate spreads evenly over the rice mixture.
5. Place the tray in the freezer until candies are set, about 30 minutes.
6. Serve chilled.

Per Serving

calories: 184 | fat: 12.1g | carbs:15.2g | protein: 3.3g | fiber: 2.1g

Homemade Almond Joys

Prep time: 5 minutes | Cook time: 1 minute | Serves 6

- ½ cup finely shredded unsweetened dried coconut
- ¼ cup unsweetened coconut milk
- 2 tablespoons almond flour
- ¼ teaspoon coconut sugar
- ½ cup dairy-free dark chocolate chips
- 18 almonds

1. Line a standard size 6-cup muffin pan with paper baking cups. Set aside. In a small bowl, combine the dried coconut, unsweetened coconut milk, almond flour, and coconut sugar. Stir until well mixed.
2. Using a tablespoon measure, divide the coconut mixture into 6 balls, and flatten them with your hand to create patties. Place in the freezer while preparing the melted chocolate.

3. In a small saucepan or double boiler, melt the chocolate over medium-low heat. Stir continuously until fully melted, about 1 minute. Add about 1 teaspoon of melted chocolate to each of the 6 baking cups. Tilt the pan until the bottoms of the cups are fully coated with chocolate.
4. Remove the coconut patties from the freezer and place one in each cup on top of the chocolate. (The patty should be almost the same diameter as the baking cup.) Place 3 almonds on top of each coconut patty. Finish by pouring the rest of the chocolate over the almonds and coconut. Tilt and gently shake the pan to spread the chocolate evenly.
5. Place in the freezer until set, about 30 minutes.
6. Serve chilled.

Per Serving

calories: 179 | fat: 14.2g | carbs:11.1g | protein: 2.3g | fiber: 3.2g

Chocolate Quinoa Bars

Prep time: 10 minutes | Cook time: 25 minutes | Makes 12 bars

- 1½ cups uncooked quinoa
- ½ cup ground almonds
- ½ cup grated or shredded dried coconut
- ½ cup dried cranberries
- ½ cup dried apples or other dried fruit, chopped
- ¼ teaspoon salt
- ½ cup almond or peanut butter
- 2 tablespoons coconut oil
- ¼ cup agave
- ½ cup chocolate chips or dark chocolate pieces

1. Preheat the oven to 350ºF (180ºC).
2. Spread the quinoa on a cookie sheet and toast for 7 to 8 minutes.
3. In a large bowl, combine the toasted quinoa, almonds, coconut, and dried fruit.
4. In a saucepan, combine the remaining ingredients, except for the chocolate chips. Bring to a simmer over medium heat for 2 minutes.
5. Pour over quinoa mixture and combine until dry ingredients are evenly coated.
6. Mix in chocolate chips.
7. Spoon into a greased baking dish. Press mixture into pan. Bake for 15 minutes.
8. Let cool and then cut and serve or store in an airtight container.

Per Serving

calories: 299 | fat: 16.9g | carbs:31.8g | protein: 6.9g | fiber: 5.2g

Chapter 9

Staples, Sauces and Dressings

110	Chickpea and White Bean Hummus
110	Lentil and Jalapeño Dip
111	Peach-Strawberry Vinaigrette
111	Balsamic Rasberry Dressing
111	Lemony Tahini Sauce
112	Sunflower Seed Parmesan "Cheese"
112	Lemony Poppy Seed Dressing
113	Raw Cashew Ricotta "Cheese"
113	Date-Cashew Sour Cream
114	Easy Vodka Sauce
114	Fast and Easy Peanut Sauce
115	Fresh Basil Pesto Sauce
115	Lemony Almond Ricotta
116	White Bean and Basil Spread
116	Quinoa with Peas and Cabbage
117	One-Pot Vegan Marinara
117	Vegan Bouillon Powder

Staples, Sauces and Dressings| 109

Chickpea and White Bean Hummus

Prep time: 5 minutes | Cook time: 0 minutes | Makes 3 cups

- 1 (15-ounce / 425-g) can chickpeas
- 1 (15-ounce / 425-g) can white beans (cannellini or great northern)
- 3 tablespoons freshly squeezed lemon juice
- 2 teaspoons garlic powder
- 1 teaspoon onion powder

1. Drain and rinse the chickpeas and white beans.
2. In a food processor or blender, combine the chickpeas, beans, lemon juice, garlic powder, and onion powder. Process for 1 to 2 minutes, or until the texture is smooth and creamy.
3. Serve immediately, or store in a refrigerator-safe container for up to 5 days.

Per Serving (½ cup)

calories: 69 | fat: 1.0g | carbs: 12.0g | protein: 4.0g | fiber: 4.0g

Lentil and Jalapeño Dip

Prep time: 5 minutes | Cook time: 22 to 27 minutes | Serves 4

- 2 cups water
- ½ cup dried brown or green lentils, rinsed
- 1 jalapeño pepper, stemmed
- ½ cup plant-based sour cream
- 1 (4-ounce / 113-g) can diced green chiles
- 1 teaspoon onion powder
- ½ teaspoon garlic powder

1. Preheat the broiler.
2. In an 8-quart pot over high heat, bring the water to a boil. Add the lentils, reduce the heat to maintain a simmer, cover the pot, and cook for 15 to 20 minutes. The lentils should be soft and squishable. Drain and set aside.
3. While the lentils cook, wrap the jalapeño pepper in aluminum foil to prevent it from burning. Place it under the broiler for 5 minutes. Turn the jalapeño pepper and cook for 2 minutes more. Remove and set aside.
4. In a high-speed blender or food processor, combine the cooked lentils, roasted jalapeño pepper, plant-based sour cream, green chiles, onion powder, and garlic powder. Purée until the dip achieves desired smoothness.
5. Serve warm or cold with chips, pita, spread on a wrap, or as a dip for crudités, as desired.

Per Serving

calories: 178 | fat: 7.2g | carbs: 21.1g | protein: 9.2g | fiber: 5.3g

Peach-Strawberry Vinaigrette

Prep time: 5 minutes | Cook time: 0 minutes | Makes 1¼ cups

- 1 peach, pitted
- 4 strawberries
- ¼ cup water
- 2 tablespoons balsamic vinegar

1. In a blender, combine the peach, strawberries, water, and vinegar. Blend on high for 1 to 2 minutes, or until the dressing has a smooth consistency.
2. Store in a refrigerator-safe container for up to 3 days.

Per Serving (2 tablespoons)

calories: 8 | fat: 0g | carbs: 2.0g | protein: 0g | fiber: 0g

Balsamic Rasberry Dressing

Prep time: 5 minutes | Cook time: 0 minutes | Serves 5

- 1 cup fresh raspberries
- 2 tablespoons raspberry vinegar
- 1 tablespoon regular or golden balsamic vinegar
- 2 tablespoons water
- 2 teaspoons liquid sweetener
- 2 teaspoons Dijon mustard
- Freshly ground pepper, to taste

1. Combine all the ingredients in a food processor and blend well.

Per Serving

calories: 23 | fat: 0g | carbs: 5.1g | protein: 0.6g | fiber: 1.1g

Lemony Tahini Sauce

Prep time: 5 minutes | Cook time: 0 minutes | Serves 2

- 2 tablespoons tahini
- 2 garlic cloves, chopped
- 1 tablespoon chopped ginger
- Juice of ½ to 1 lemon
- 2 tablespoons nutritional yeast
- 1 tablespoon soy sauce
- Water, as needed

1. Place all the ingredients into a blender or food processor.
2. Blend until smooth, adding water as needed.

Per Serving

calories: 148 | fat: 9.1g | carbs: 11.2g | protein: 11.3g | fiber: 6.1g

Sunflower Seed Parmesan "Cheese"

Prep time: 5 minutes | Cook time: 0 minutes | Makes ½ cup

- ½ cup sunflower seeds
- 2 tablespoons nutritional yeast
- ½ teaspoon garlic powder

1. In a food processor or blender, combine the sunflower seeds, nutritional yeast, and garlic powder. Process on low for 30 to 45 seconds, or until the sunflower seeds have been broken down to the size of coarse sea salt.
2. Store in a refrigerator-safe container for up to 2 months.

Per Serving (1 tablespoon)

calories: 56 | fat: 4.0g | carbs: 3.0g | protein: 3.0g | fiber: 1.0g

Lemony Poppy Seed Dressing

Prep time: 5 minutes | Cook time: 5 minutes | Makes 1 cup

- ½ cup plant-based milk
- 2 tablespoons freshly squeezed lemon juice
- 1 tablespoon apple cider vinegar
- 1 tablespoon maple syrup
- 2 teaspoons dried poppy seeds
- 2 teaspoons cornstarch
- ½ teaspoon garlic powder

1. In a small saucepan, combine the milk, lemon juice, vinegar, maple syrup, poppy seeds, cornstarch, and garlic powder. Mix until the cornstarch has completely dissolved.
2. Place the pan over medium heat and bring the dressing to a rolling boil, about 5 minutes. Whisk the dressing, then remove from the heat.
3. Allow the dressing to cool before storing in a refrigerator-safe container for up to 4 days.

Per Serving (2 tablespoons)

calories: 18 | fat: 1.0g | carbs: 3.0g | protein: 0g | fiber: 0g

Raw Cashew Ricotta "Cheese"

Prep time: 5 minutes | Cook time: 0 minutes | Makes 1½ cups

- 1½ cups raw cashews
- 1 garlic clove
- Juice of 1 lemon
- 1 tablespoon nutritional yeast
- ½ teaspoon salt, plus more to taste
- ¼ teaspoon freshly ground black pepper

1. Place the cashews in a heatproof bowl and add boiling water to cover. Let soak for 10 minutes before draining (reserve the soaking liquid).
2. Place the drained cashews in a food processor along with ½ cup of the soaking liquid. Blend for 30 seconds until combined. Scrape down the sides of the bowl. Add the garlic, lemon juice, nutritional yeast, salt, and pepper. Blend for 2 to 3 minutes until creamy.
3. Taste and add more salt if needed. Ricotta should be a little salty, so add salt to your liking and blend once more.
4. Serve.

Per Serving (¼ cup)

calories: 194 | fat: 14.0g | carbs: 10.0g | protein: 7.0g | fiber: 1.0g

Date-Cashew Sour Cream

Prep time: 5 minutes | Cook time: 0 minutes | Makes 1¼ cups

- 1 cup raw cashews
- 1 garlic clove
- ½ pitted Medjool date
- Juice of ½ lemon, or more to taste
- ½ cup water, plus more as needed

1. Place the cashews in a heatproof bowl and add boiling water to cover. Let soak for 10 minutes before draining (discard the soaking liquid).
2. In a food processor, combine the cashews, garlic, date, and lemon juice. Blend for 30 to 60 seconds until combined.
3. Slowly add ½ cup water, blending for 2 to 3 minutes or until the mixture is smooth and similar to sour cream in consistency. Taste and add more lemon juice, if needed.
4. Serve.

Per Serving (2 tablespoons)

calories: 87 | fat: 7.0g | carbs: 4.0g | protein: 2.0g | fiber: 1.0g

Easy Vodka Sauce

Prep time: 5 minutes | Cook time: 7 minutes | Makes 3 cups

- ¾ cup raw cashews
- ¼ cup boiling water
- 1 tablespoon olive oil
- 4 garlic cloves, minced
- 1½ cups unsweetened almond milk
- 1 tablespoon arrowroot powder
- 1 teaspoon salt
- 1 tablespoon nutritional yeast
- 1¼ cups marinara sauce

1. Place the cashews in a heatproof bowl and add boiling water to cover. Let soak for 10 minutes. Drain the cashews and place them in a blender. Add ¼ cup boiling water and blend for 1 to 2 minutes or until creamy. Set aside.
2. In a small saucepan, heat the olive oil over medium heat. Add the garlic and sauté for 2 minutes, until golden. Whisk in the almond milk, arrowroot powder, and salt. Bring to a simmer. Continue to simmer, whisking frequently, for about 5 minutes or until the sauce thickens.
3. Carefully transfer the hot almond milk mixture to the blender with the cashews. Blend for 30 seconds to combine, then add the nutritional yeast and marinara sauce. Blend for 1 minute or until creamy.
4. Serve.

Per Serving (¾ cup)

calories: 267 | fat: 19.0g | carbs: 15.0g | protein: 9.0g | fiber: 4.0g

Fast and Easy Peanut Sauce

Prep time: 5 minutes | Cook time: 0 minutes | Serves 4

- ½ cup peanut butter
- 1 to 2 tablespoons soy sauce
- 2 teaspoons rice vinegar
- 1 tablespoon maple syrup
- 2 to 4 cloves garlic
- 1 tablespoon-sized piece of fresh ginger or 1 teaspoon powdered ginger
- Sriracha or other hot sauce, to taste (optional)
- ½ cup low-sodium vegetable broth

1. Combine all the ingredients, except for the broth, in a blender and blend until smooth. Add the vegetable broth until desired consistency is reached.

Per Serving

calories: 217 | fat: 17.2g | carbs: 12.3g | protein: 8.3g | fiber: 2.1g

Fresh Basil Pesto Sauce

Prep time: 5 minutes | Cook time: 0 minutes | Makes 24 tablespoons

- 3 cups packed fresh basil leaves
- 3 to 4 cloves garlic
- ⅓ cup pine nuts, lightly toasted
- ⅓ cup olive oil
- ¼ cup nutritional yeast
- ¼ teaspoon salt
- ⅛ teaspoon cayenne pepper
- Cooked pasta, for serving

1. Place the basil leaves and garlic in a blender or food processor and mince well.
2. Add the pine nuts and continue to blend until nuts and basil are ground.
3. Drizzle in the olive oil, as you keep the machine running, until mixture becomes a fine paste.
4. Transfer to a bowl and stir in the nutritional yeast. Season with salt and pepper.
5. Toss over hot pasta and serve immediately.

Per Serving (1 tablespoon)

calories: 45 | fat: 4.4g | carbs: 1.2g | protein: 1.1g | fiber: 0.4g

Lemony Almond Ricotta

Prep time: 5 minutes | Cook time: 0 minutes | Makes 1 cup

- 2 cups blanched slivered almonds
- ¾ cup cold water
- 2 tablespoons freshly squeezed lemon juice
- 1 tablespoon lemon zest
- 1 tablespoon pure maple syrup
- 2 teaspoons nutritional yeast
- ½ teaspoon almond extract

1. In a food processor or high-speed blender, combine the almonds, water, lemon juice, lemon zest, maple syrup, nutritional yeast, and almond extract. Pulse to combine, scrape down the sides, and purée until mostly smooth.
2. Refrigerate in an airtight container for up to 2 weeks, or freeze for up to 6 months.

Per Serving (2 tablespoons)

calories: 167 | fat: 14.2g | carbs: 8.1g | protein: 6.3g | fiber: 4.0g

White Bean and Basil Spread

Prep time: 5 minutes | Cook time: 0 minutes | Serves 8

- 2 (15-ounce / 425 g) cans white beans, rinsed and drained
- Juice of ½ lemon
- 1 bunch fresh basil
- Pinch of salt
- Pinch of black pepper
- 2 tablespoons nutritional yeast
- 1 small red onion, thinly diced

1. In a medium bowl, combine the beans, lemon juice, basil, salt, pepper, and nutritional yeast. Roughly mash the mixture with the back of a fork.
2. Fold in the chopped red onion to the mixture.

Per Serving

calories: 138 | fat: 0g | carbs: 25.2g | protein: 10.1g | fiber: 6.2g

Quinoa with Peas and Cabbage

Prep time: 5 minutes | Cook time: 15 minutes | Serves 8

- 2 cups quinoa, rinsed
- 3 cups water or vegetable broth
- 1 cup frozen peas
- 1 cup diced red cabbage
- Salt, to taste

1. Add all the ingredients to a medium-sized pot over medium heat and bring to a boil.
2. Turn heat to low, let simmer for 15 minutes, or until the liquid is absorbed and the quinoa is cooked through.
3. Serve warm

Per Serving

calories: 101 | fat: 1.2g | carbs: 18.2g | protein: 4.3g | fiber: 3.2g

One-Pot Vegan Marinara

Prep time: 5 minutes | Cook time: 10 minutes | Makes 2¼ cups

- 1 cup water
- 1 cup tomato paste
- 2 tablespoons maple syrup
- 1 teaspoon dried oregano
- 1 teaspoon dried thyme
- 1 teaspoon garlic powder
- 1 teaspoon onion powder
- ½ teaspoon dried basil
- ¼ teaspoon red pepper flakes

1. In a medium saucepan, bring the water to a boil over high heat. Reduce the heat to low, and whisk in the tomato paste, maple syrup, oregano, thyme, garlic powder, onion powder, basil, and red pepper flakes.
2. Cover and simmer for 10 minutes, stirring occasionally. Serve warm.

Per Serving (½ cup)
calories: 69 | fat: 0g | carbs: 17.0g | protein: 3.0g | fiber: 3.0g

Vegan Bouillon Powder

Prep time: 5 minutes | Cook time: 0 minutes | Makes 2 cups

- 2 cups nutritional yeast
- ¼ cup sea salt (optional)
- 2 tablespoons onion powder
- 1 tablespoon Italian seasoning
- 2 teaspoons garlic powder
- 1 teaspoon ground turmeric
- 1 teaspoon celery salt
- 1 teaspoon dried thyme

1. In a small blender or food processor, combine the nutritional yeast, salt (if using), onion powder, Italian seasoning, garlic powder, turmeric, celery salt, and thyme. Blend to a powder.
2. Store the bouillon powder in a sealable jar or container at room temperature. Use 1 tablespoon per 1 cup of water for a flavorful stock.

Per Serving (1 tablespoon)
calories: 24 | fat: 0g | carbs: 3.1g | protein: 3.3g | fiber: 1.2g

Appendix 1: Measurement Conversion Chart

VOLUME EQUIVALENTS (DRY)

US STANDARD	METRIC (APPROXIMATE)
1/8 teaspoon	0.5 mL
1/4 teaspoon	1 mL
1/2 teaspoon	2 mL
3/4 teaspoon	4 mL
1 teaspoon	5 mL
1 tablespoon	15 mL
1/4 cup	59 mL
1/2 cup	118 mL
3/4 cup	177 mL
1 cup	235 mL
2 cups	475 mL
3 cups	700 mL
4 cups	1 L

VOLUME EQUIVALENTS (LIQUID)

US STANDARD	US STANDARD (OUNCES)	METRIC (APPROXIMATE)
2 tablespoons	1 fl.oz.	30 mL
1/4 cup	2 fl.oz.	60 mL
1/2 cup	4 fl.oz.	120 mL
1 cup	8 fl.oz.	240 mL
1 1/2 cup	12 fl.oz.	355 mL
2 cups or 1 pint	16 fl.oz.	475 mL
4 cups or 1 quart	32 fl.oz.	1 L
1 gallon	128 fl.oz.	4 L

TEMPERATURES EQUIVALENTS

FAHRENHEIT(F)	CELSIUS(C) (APPROXIMATE)
225 °F	107 °C
250 °F	120 °C
275 °F	135 °C
300 °F	150 °C
325 °F	160 °C
350 °F	180 °C
375 °F	190 °C
400 °F	205 °C
425 °F	220 °C
450 °F	235 °C
475 °F	245 °C
500 °F	260 °C

WEIGHT EQUIVALENTS

US STANDARD	METRIC (APPROXIMATE)
1 ounce	28 g
2 ounces	57 g
5 ounces	142 g
10 ounces	284 g
15 ounces	425 g
16 ounces (1 pound)	455 g
1.5 pounds	680 g
2 pounds	907 g

Appendix 2: Recipe Index

A
Air-Fried Seitan   66
Almond Protein Shake   35
Apple and Cinnamon Smoothie   36
Apple and Walnut Bowl   40
Asian Noodles with Nutty Tofu Crisp   67
Avocado-Strawberry Toast   79

B
5-Bean Chili   64
Baked Fruit Crisp   105
Balsamic Rasberry Dressing   111
Banana and Blueberry Smoothie   44
Banana and Oat Pancakes   35
Bananas and Peanut Butter Smoothie   37
Black Bean and Avocado Salad   64
Braised Chipotle Tacos   91
Breakfast Burrito   37
Breakfast Skillet   41
Brown Rice and Black Bean Burritos   71

C
Carrot, Barley and Spinach Soup   85
Cauliflower Rice with Satay Tempeh   55
Cherry-Chocolate Ice Cream   104
Chickpea and Spinach Salad   63
Chickpea and White Bean Hummus   110
Chocolate Chia Pudding   39
Chocolate Cookies   103
Chocolate Quinoa Bars   107
Chocolate Sunflower Seed Balls   82
Chocolate-Banana Smoothie Bowl   45
Cinnamon-Vanilla French Toast   46
Citrus Kale Salad   49
Classic Chana Masala   57
Classic Coconut Tofu Curry   99

Coconut Lemon Protein Bites   82
Cookie Dough Oats   77
Couscous Salad with Chickpeas   53
Cranberry-Pear Polenta   39
Crispy Baked Tempeh   73
Crispy Cauliflower Florets   79
Crispy Kale Chips   78

D
Date and Walnut Chocolate Balls   104
Date-Cashew Sour Cream   113

E
Easy Vodka Sauce   114
Edamame and Asparagus Risotto   93

F
Farro Bowl with Kidney Beans   58
Fast and Easy Corn Salsa   84
Fast and Easy Peanut Sauce   114
Fresh Basil Pesto Sauce   115
Fresh Mango Salsa   83

G
Garlic-Maple Air-Fried Tofu   89
Golden Tofu Brown Rice Bowl   49

H
Hearty Vegetable Pie   94
Homemade Almond Joys   106

K
Kale Slaw Tacos   68
Kiwi-Strawberry Chia Pudding   34

L
Leek and Asparagus Soup   86
Lemony Almond Ricotta   115
Lemony Poppy Seed Dressing   112
Lemony Tahini Sauce   111

Lentil and Jalapeño Dip   110
Lentil and Kale Stew   76

M
Mac 'N' Mince   58
Mango and Orange Smoothie   44
Mango Quinoa Bowl with Tempeh   51
Microwave Chocolate Mug Cake   102
Mocha Chocolate Brownie Bars   78
Mushroom and Tofu Scramble   96

O
Oatmeal and Currant Energy Balls   105
Oatmeal Protein Shake   38
One-Pot Vegan Marinara   117
Orange and Strawberry Smoothie   34

O
Papaya and Mango Smoothie Cubes   40
Pasta with Ricotta Red Sauce   72
Peach-Strawberry Vinaigrette   111
Peanut Butter Protein Balls   103
Peanut Butter Scotcheroos   106
Peanut Oatmeal Cookies   80
Peppermint-Chocolate Nice Cream   81
Pesto Pasta Salad   52
Pistachio Energy Bites   80
Plantain Mango Nice Cream   83
Potato Lentil Soup   91

Q
Quinoa Bowl with Basil Pesto   50
Quinoa with Peas and Cabbage   116

R
Raw Cashew Ricotta "Cheese"   113

S
Sesame Tempeh in Soy Sauce   56
Simple Chickpea Guacamole   84
Simple Chickpea Salad Sandwich   63
Simple Sushi Bowl   90
Smoked Tofu and Black Beans Bowl   59

Soba Noodles with Tempeh   60
Soya Mince and Noodle Bowl   98
Spiced Split Pea Soup   77
Spiced Sweet Potato Cake   102
Spiced Veggie Fajitas   72
Spicy Soba Noodles with Peanut Sauce   70
Stacked Portobello Burgers   54
Stuffed Avocado   53
Sumptuous Buddha Bowl   65
Sumptuous Minestrone Soup   90
Sunflower Seed Parmesan "Cheese"   112
Sushi Bowl with Veggies   50
Sweet Potato and Broccoli Bowl   56

T
Tacos with Tempeh and Baked Cauliflower   69
Teriyaki Tempeh Lettuce Wraps   52
Teriyaki Veggies and Tofu   96
Tofu and Spinach Breakfast Scramble   36
Tofu and Veggie Brown Rice Bowl   92
Tofu Club Wrap   51
Tofu Pita with Tzatziki Sauce   95

V
Vanilla Banana Smoothie   45
Vegan BLT Sandwich   97
Vegan Bouillon Powder   117
Vegan Meat-Free Loaf   98
Vegan Meatballs over Spaghetti   92
Vegan Mushroom Omelet   38
Veggie Hummus Pizza   89
Veggie-Loaded Baked Sweet Potatoes   76

W
Walnut Cranberry Power Cookies   81
White Bean and Basil Spread   116

Z
Zoodles with Crunchy Sesame Tofu   66

References

Gerard, J. (n.d.). Can Your Vegan Athletes Match Their Meat-eating Competitors? ACE Fitness. Retrieved September 12, 2020, from https://www.acefitness.org/certifiednewsarticle/3100/can-your-vegan-athletes-match-their-meat-eating-competitors/#:~:text=In%20the%20minds%20of%20many

Krantz, R. (2016, February 15). 8 Reasons Meat Is Bad For You. Bustle. https://www.bustle.com/articles/137865-8-reasons-meat-is-bad-for-you-yes-even-chicken

Petre, A. (2019, October 15). 7 Supplements You Need on a Vegan Diet. Healthline. https://www.healthline.com/nutrition/7-supplements-for-vegans#10

Weatherwax-Fall, D. (n.d.). Different Nutritional Plans for Different Athletes. NSCA's Performance Training Journal, 5(6). Retrieved September 11, 2020, from https://athletics.macalester.edu/custompages/Deno_Videos/nutrition/nutrition_plans.pdf

Printed in Great Britain
by Amazon